D1027014

VOLUME 20 IS ABOUT
THIS GIRL!
TEE HEE!
T
ASUMI

Finally! We made it to volume 20!

In human years, it's the age when you're allowed to drink alcohol in Japan!

Thank you so much for sticking with us all this way!

In honor of this landmark occasion, I recently started a YouTube channel to practice drawing and to get more exposure.

Whenever I show it to my daughter, who likes watching videos, she always wants to change the channel after one second. But I will survive!

Anyway, in this volume we begin the story of a certain senpai…if this 'n' that 'n' that other thing had happened…

I hope you enjoy it!

Taishi Tsutsui

We Never Learn

We Never Learn

Volume 20 • SHONEN JUMP Manga Edition

STORY AND ART **Taishi Tsutsui**

TRANSLATION Camellia Nieh

SHONEN JUMP SERIES LETTERING Snir Aharon

GRAPHIC NOVEL TOUCH-UP ART & LETTERING Erika Terriquez

DESIGN Shawn Carrico

EDITOR John Bae

Printed in Canada

Published by VIZ Media, LLC
P.O. Box 77010
San Francisco, CA 94107

10 9 8 7 6 5 4 3 2 1
First printing, February 2022

PARENTAL ADVISORY
WE NEVER LEARN is rated T+ for Older Teen and is recommended for ages 16 and up. This volume contains mild language and sexual themes.

[x] We + Never ÷ × Learn
20
[X] = Tomorrow Night's Pixie
Taishi Tsutsui

We Never Learn

Characters & Story

Nariyuki Yuiga and his family have led a humble life since his father passed away, with Yuiga doing everything he can to support his siblings. So when the principal of his school agrees to grant Nariyuki the school's special VIP recommendation for a full scholarship to college, he leaps at the opportunity. However, the principal's offer comes with one condition: Yuiga must serve as the tutor of Rizu Ogata, Fumino Furuhashi and Uruka Takemoto, the three girl geniuses who are the pride of Ichinose Academy! Unfortunately, the girls, while extremely talented in certain ways, all have subjects where their grades are absolutely rock-bottom.

Now that everyone has passed their exams, what will happen in the future?! According to a school legend, the moment the first firework explodes on the night of the school festival, any boy and girl who are touching are destined to end up together. These alternate realities follow the parallel pathways that diverge from that moment!

NARIYUKI YUIGA

- ☺ Liberal Arts
- ☺ STEM
- ☹ Athletics

A bright student from an ordinary family. Nariyuki lacks genius in any one subject but manages to maintain stellar grades through hard work. After taking on the role of tutor to Rizu, Fumino, and Uruka, he decides to pursue a teaching degree.

ASUMI KOMINAMI

- ☺ STEM
- ☺ Service

A graduate of Ichinose Academy. She is aiming to get into medical school to take over her father's clinic one day.

Kasumi Kominami

Asumi's mother. A brilliant surgeon who often works overseas.

Sojiro Kominami

Asumi's father. Runs his own medical clinic.

Fumino Furuhashi

Known as the Sleeping Beauty of the Literary Forest, Fumino is a literary wiz. She chooses a STEM path because she wants to study the stars.

Uruka Takemoto

Known as the Shimmering Ebony Mermaid Princess, Uruka is a swimming prodigy and is currently studying abroad.

Mafuyu Kirisu

A teacher at Ichinose Academy, and Rizu and Fumino's former tutor.

Rizu Ogata

Known as the Thumbelina Supercomputer, Rizu is a math and science genius, but she's a dunce at literature, especially when human emotions come into play. She chooses a literary path to learn about human psychology—partially because she wants to become better at board games.

TITLE

We Never Learn

CONTENTS

VOLUME **20** [*X*] = Tomorrow Night's Pixie

NAME **Taishi Tsutsui**

Question 169:
[X] = Tomorrow Night's Pixie, Part 1

HEY, KOHAI ...

WHAT IF WE REALLY DO END UP TOGETHER?

Route: 4/5 [X] = Tomorrow Night's Pixie

SEVERAL YEARS LATER...

WELL ...

WE HAVE A NEW TEACHER TODAY...

...FROM THE MAIN-LAND...

...

ER ...

WHAT WAS YOUR NAME AGAIN?

OH!

MY NAME IS YUIGA.
I'LL BE YOUR TEACHER STARTING TODAY!
NARIYUKI YUIGA
HONESTLY, I JUST ARRIVED ON THE ISLAND BY BOAT THIS MORNING...
...SO I HOPE YOU'LL HELP ME LEARN ABOUT THIS PLACE.
HEH HEH...
NO FAIR, TAICHI!
THERE'S NO CUTE GUYS ON THIS ISLAND!
BLUSH
YAY! IT'S YOUR TREAT AT THE STORE AFTER SCHOOL TODAY!
YAP YAP
YAP YAP
YAP YAP
YAP
YAP
THERE AREN'T SO MANY KIDS ON THIS ISLAND, SO...
CHATTER CHATTER
...WE JUST PUT THE GRADE SCHOOL AND JUNIOR HIGH KIDS TOGETHER IN ONE CLASS. I'M SURE YOU CAN HANDLE IT...
YAP
...
WELL, I'M GLAD THEY SEEM LIKE A LIVELY GROUP...

FACULTY
GOODNESS!
AIN'T IT A BLESSING TO HAVE SUCH A YOUNG TEACHER COME HERE FROM THE MAINLAND!
I'm the principal!
I'm the vice-principal!
IT'S JUST US OLD FOLKS HERE.
IT'S BEEN A STRUGGLE TO LOOK AFTER ALL THEM ROWDY KIDS!
OH! I SEE...
WELL, I'M THRILLED TO BE OF SERVICE!
THUMP THUMP
SHK SHK
NOW, NO NEED TO BE SO POLITE!
Have some rice crackers.
MAINLANDERS SURE ARE FORMAL!
SPEAKING OF FORMAL, HOW ABOUT THAT CUTE NEW DOCTOR WHO RECENTLY JOINED US?
YEAH, SHE WAS PRETTY NERVOUS AT FIRST TOO!
YAP YAP YAP YAP
...
TWO YEARS HAVE PASSED SINCE I GRADUATED UNIVERSITY.
IT'S BEEN QUITE THE JOURNEY...
...TO THIS TEACHING POST ON A SMALL, REMOTE ISLAND.
BUT STILL...

I FORE-SEE...
...PLENTY OF CHAL-LENGES AHEAD.
HUFF! HUFF!
WOBBLE
WOBBLE
I DIDN'T REALIZE IT WAS THREE KILO-METERS TO THE GUEST-HOUSE!
PROBABLY SHOULD HAVE SHIPPED MY BAG...
SHF SHF
HUFF...
SWELTER
I'M DYING.
IT'S SO HOT... IS IT REALLY SPRING?
SWELTER
SWELTER
SLUMP
!
STARE
HEY, SHE'S ONE OF MY STUDENTS...
I THINK HER NAME IS YUKARI SHIMA.
WOBBLE
WOBBLE
SLUMP
?!
HEY! SHIMA?!
AFTERNOON HOMEWRECKER

HUH?
I...
DID YOU...
...DRAG ME TO THE GROUND, SENSEI?
GRAB
Huff
Huff
NO, THE OPPOSITE!
THAT SOUNDS SO BAD... PLEASE DON'T SAY THAT!
PLUNK

KLATTER
S...
S...
DA DA DUM
K...
K...
DA DA DA DA
SENPAI?! KOMINAMI SENPAI?!
WHAAAAAT?!
KO-HAI?!
WHAT ARE YOU DOING HERE?!

HEH
WELL, WELL!
WE HEARD THERE WAS A NEW TEACHER ON THE ISLAND, BUT WE HAD NO IDEA IT WAS YOU, YUIGA!
IT MUST BE DESTINY! ♪

Y-YOU TOO, MS. KASUMI?!
WHAT IS GOING ON?!
THIS IS ONE OF THE CLINICS I RUN. ♡
STARE
Aaah
Aaah
What a crazy coincidence...
WHAAAAT?!
AND I...
...ASKED MY MOM TO LET ME DO MY RESIDENCY HERE.
RESIDENCY?

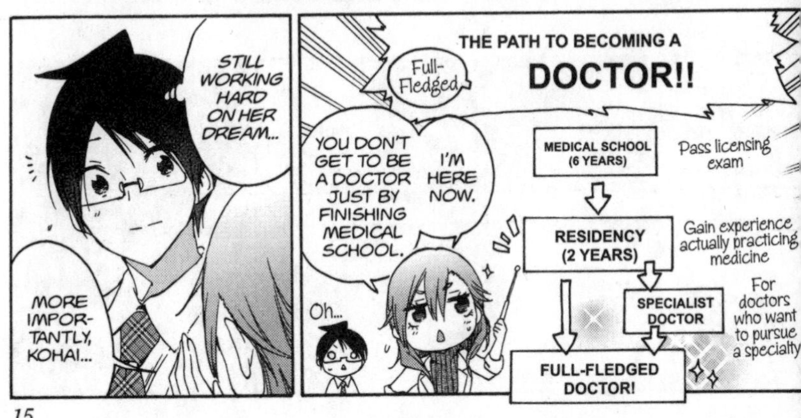
THE PATH TO BECOMING A Full-Fledged DOCTOR!!
MEDICAL SCHOOL (6 YEARS)
Pass licensing exam
RESIDENCY (2 YEARS)
Gain experience actually practicing medicine
SPECIALIST DOCTOR
For doctors who want to pursue a specialty
FULL-FLEDGED DOCTOR!
I'M HERE NOW.
YOU DON'T GET TO BE A DOCTOR JUST BY FINISHING MEDICAL SCHOOL.
Oh...
STILL WORKING HARD ON HER DREAM...
MORE IMPORTANTLY, KOHAI...

WE HAVEN'T SEEN EACH OTHER IN A WHILE...
AREN'T YOU GOING TO TELL ME I LOOK PRETTY?

WHERE DID THAT COME FROM?!
HEE HEE HEE!
WHY ARE YOU TURNING RED? YOU'RE AS ADORABLE AS EVER! ♡
PSST
PSST

DON'T TELL ME YOU'RE ALREADY HITTING ON STUDENTS ON YOUR FIRST DAY...
That's not cool!
I'M NOT HITTING ON STUDENTS!
GRRR
?

PHEW... IT'S REALLY DARK OUT NOW...
I DIDN'T THINK IT WOULD BE THAT FAR TO SHIMA'S HOUSE...
Koff
GLAD TO HEAR IT WAS JUST A COLD.

...
ASUMI!
DO YOU REALLY THINK YOU CAN SEW UP A PATIENT WITH STITCHES LIKE THESE?
MORE PRAC-TICE!

R-RIGHT!
YES, MOTHER...
I MEAN, DOC-TOR!

WOW...
I CAN'T BELIEVE WE END-ED UP ON THE SAME LITTLE ISLAND.

AREN'T YOU GOING TO TELL ME I LOOK PRETTY?

...
WELL, YEAH.
SEEMS LIKE SHE DID GET PRETTIER.

BUT IT'S TRUE...
... YOU SUP-PORTED ME A LOT.

MAYBE I REALLY SHOULD GIVE YOU A KISS THIS TIME.
YEAH, SURE.
I'M NOT FALLING FOR THAT ONE AGAIN.

YOU KNOW, KOHAI...
THE LEGEND OF THE SCHOOL FESTIVAL...
DO YOU REMEMBER IT?

WHAT IF...
...WE REALLY DO END UP TOGETHER?
...

WAIT, WHY AM I THINKING ABOUT THAT?!
I'VE GOT TO FOCUS ON STARTING TEACHING TOMORROW!
WHRR
WHRR

WOW ...
WHAT A NICE, BIG ROOM!
TA DAA!
Finally made it!
THIS IS GREAT!
I CAN REALLY STRETCH OUT ON THE FLOOR! THIS IS SO NICE!
ROLL ROLL ROLL
WHEEE!
TUNK
?
WHAT'S WITH THIS PATCH OF WALL?
PAT PAT
IT FEELS KINDA WET...
PUSH PUSH
KRAKK
!

K...
S...
JOLT
K-KOHAI, WHAT ARE YOU—
FLUSTER
SLIP

FLAP

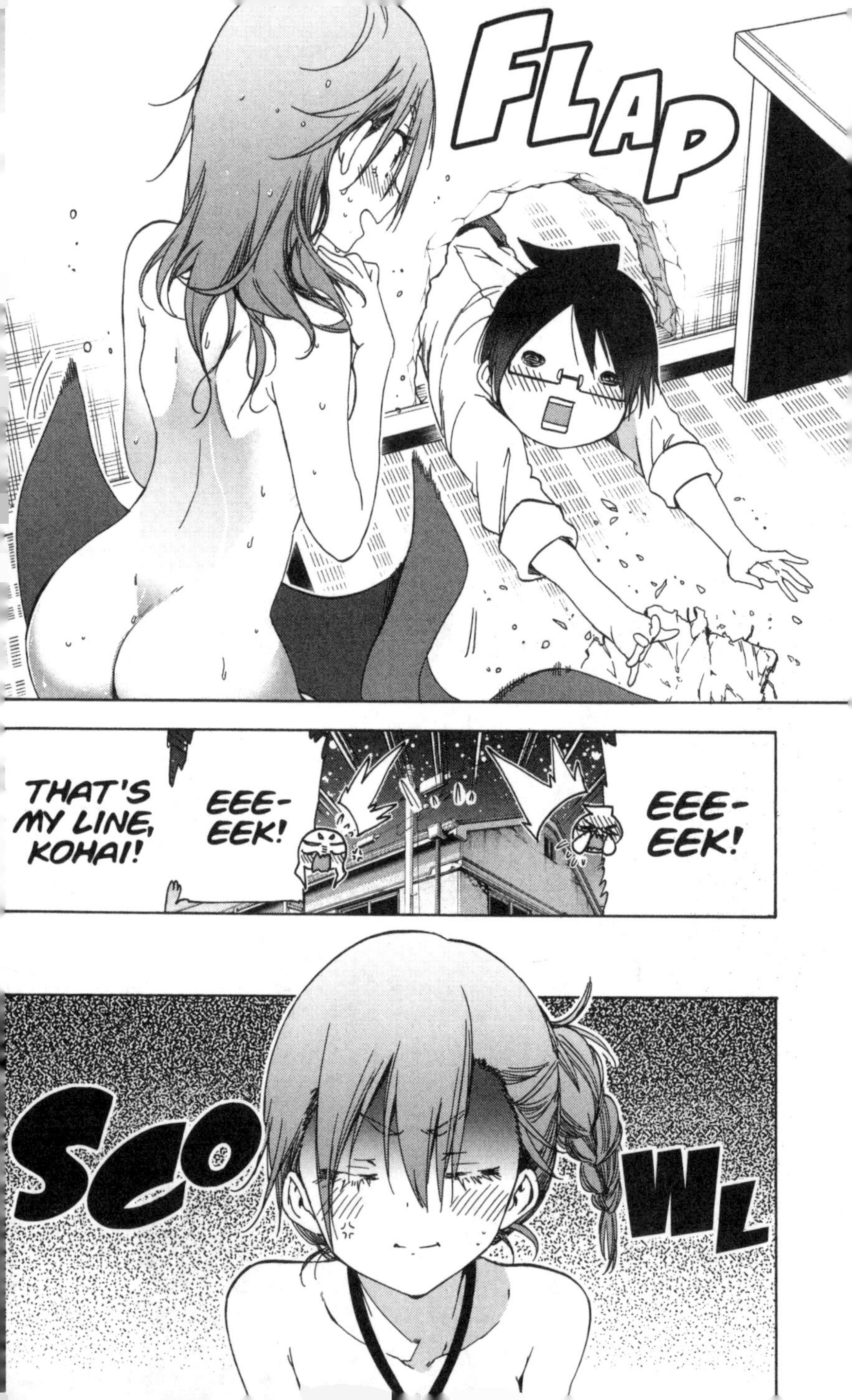

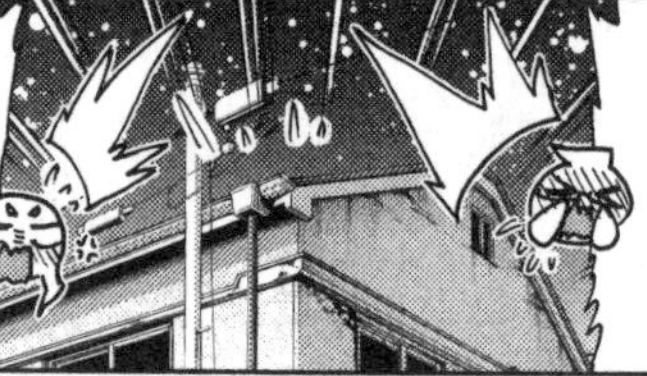

EEE-EEK!
EEE-EEK!
THAT'S MY LINE, KOHAI!

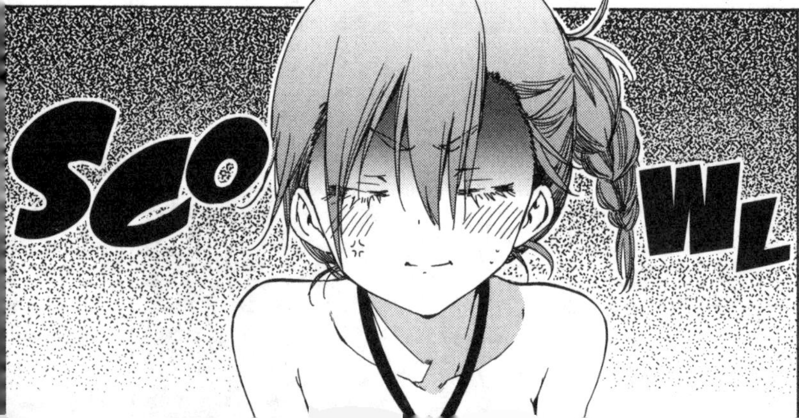

SCOWL

YOU DON'T HAVE TO KEEP APOLOGIZING.
I'M THE ONE WHO BUSTED THE WALL IN THE FIRST PLACE...
I THOUGHT I COULD JUST PUT IN SOME NEW PLASTER, BUT I GUESS THAT WAS A FAIL.
Oh no!
Tamp Tamp
I MEAN ...
IT'S ALREADY CRAZY THAT WE'RE BOTH WORKING ON THE SAME ISLAND...
...WITHOUT BEING NEXT-DOOR NEIGHBORS!
YEAH, I KNOW ...
I CAN'T BELIEVE IT...
!

UM... WHAT ARE YOU DOING THERE, SENPAI?
I'M PRACTICING MY SURGICAL STITCHING.
I'M JUST NOT VERY GOOD AT IT.
This is a practice kit!
I PRACTICE EVERY NIGHT, BUT I STILL STINK AT IT...
WOW. YOU USE THESE CLAMPS AND SCISSORS FOR SUTURING, HUH?
Looks neat!
IT'S NOT THE KIND OF THING YOU CAN JUST PICK UP IMMEDIATELY.
ANYWAY, WE'VE GOTTA FIX THAT WALL AS SOON AS POSSIBLE...
DONE!

YOU'RE RIGHT.

IT'S PAIN-STAKING WORK!

Asumi

Nariyuki

AND THAT HOLE REALLY IS A PROBLEM...

IT DOESN'T SEEM EASY TO FIX...

I WONDER IF THEY'LL GET US NEW APARTMENTS IF WE TALK TO THE SCHOOL...

CLAMP
THERE MUST ME A REASON WE'RE MEETING AGAIN LIKE THIS.
THANKS FOR MOVING IN NEXT DOOR, KOHAI, BUT...
...FORGET ABOUT THE HOLE!
MORE IMPOR-TANTLY...
WHAAAAT?!

STARTING TOMORROW...
...WHENEVER YOU HAVE TIME, MORNING OR NIGHT...
...I'D APPRECIATE IT IF YOU'D HELP ME PRACTICE AS MUCH AS POSSIBLE.

WHAT?
OF COURSE...
...IN RETURN...
I FEEL SHY ABOUT THIS...
...BUT I'LL MAKE SURE TO SHOW MY APPRECIATION...
...OKAY? ♡

WHAA-AT?!
HUH?
DON'T TELL ME YOU TOOK THAT IN A DIRTY WAY, YOU HORN-DOG!
Heh!
I DIDN'T!
AND SO...
...MY CURIOUS ISLAND JOURNEY WITH SENPAI BEGAN TO UNFOLD.

KASUMI KOMINAMI...
...STAYED IN THE CLINIC OVERNIGHT.
ZZZ
She looks surprisingly peaceful.
Yeah...

Question 170: [X] = Tomorrow Night's Pixie, Part 2

YAWN

KYAA YAAA KYAA YAAA

AH...

I SEE OUR STUDENTS ARE AS LIVELY AS EVER TODAY...
Dude, I hate getting vaccines! Whatta drag!
HEY, WE SAW THAT!
ARE TEACHERS ALLOWED TO YAWN?
OH! S-SORRY! I'M SHORT ON SLEEP!
OH!
THAT REMINDS ME!

IS IT TRUE THAT YOU'RE DATING DR. ASUMI FROM THE INFIRMARY, SENSEI?
BLRFF
Hm?

W-WHY WOULD YOU SAY THAT, SAYAKA?!
Koff
Koff
I HEARD FROM THE GRANDPA NEXT DOOR...
...THAT YOU TWO WERE ACTING AWFUL CHUMMY AT THE CLINIC!
WHA—?!

GOSH... RUMORS SURE SPREAD FAST ON AN ISLAND.
WELL, THERE'S NOTHING BETWEEN US...
THAT'S A MISUNDER-STANDING, SAYAN!

YEAH! YOU REALLY THINK SENSEI HAS A GIRLFRIEND? HE'S TOO DERPY.
...
Oh! You're right, Nao! Good point!
WELL, DON'T SUGAR-COAT IT.

ANY-WAY...
WE MAY NOT BE DATING, BUT...
...IT IS AN UNUSUAL RELATION-SHIP.

LAST NIGHT ...

KNOCK BEFORE OPENING!
SPARKLE
SPARKLE
SPARKLE
WHOA...
THIS HAS GOTTEN EASIER THANKS TO YOUR HELP.
YOU'VE REALLY PROGRESSED AT STITCHING IN THE LAST FEW DAYS!
THANKS, KOHAI.
I APPRE-CIATE YOU HELPING ME UNTIL LATE EVERY NIGHT...
One more time...
STARTING TOMORROW...
...I'D APPRECIATE IT IF YOU'D HELP ME PRACTICE AS MUCH AS POSSIBLE.
AT FIRST, I DIDN'T KNOW WHAT TO EXPECT...
...BUT IT FIGURES—SHE'S SO DRIVEN.
...
YOU KNOW, KOHAI...

I'M GLAD WE MET AGAIN.
WHEN YOU'RE AROUND ...
...SOMEHOW...
...I FEEL SAFER.

BLUSH
JUST KIDDING! DID THAT MAKE YOUR HEART RACE?
WOULD YOU CUT THAT OUT?!
TOK TOK
MR. YUIGA! PLEASE KEEP IT DOWN!
YOU DON'T HAVE COMPANY AT THIS HOUR, DO YOU?!
OH, SHOOT! THAT'S THE LANDLORD!
BETTER GO NOW BEFORE HE FINDS OUT.

HONESTLY ...
SHE HASN'T CHANGED ONE BIT.
All she does is tease me!
YAP
YAP
MYAA
IN RETURN ...
I FEEL SHY ABOUT THIS...
...BUT I'LL MAKE SURE TO SHOW MY APPRECIATION...
WHAT DID SHE MEAN ...
...BY THAT?
BADMP
BADMP
SENSEI...
!
TMP
OH ...

SHIMA
IS YOUR COLD ALL BETTER NOW?
OH. YES.
BECAUSE OF YOUR HELP THE OTHER DAY. I DIDN'T EVEN GET TO THANK YOU...
I'M SUCH A SPACE CASE ALL THE TIME...
DON'T BE SILLY, SHIMA.
Shima
I'M GLAD YOU'RE FEELING BETTER.
NEXT TIME YOU'RE FEEL-ING FUNNY, PLEASE GO TO THE CLINIC RIGHT AWAY.
STARE
?
WELL DONE, YUIGA SEN-SEI!
COMING TO THE AID OF AN AILING STUDENT!
NICE!
THUMP
?!
THERE AIN'T A HEALTH TEACHER AT THE SCHOOL...
IT'S JUST US OLD FOLKS!
WELL, GOSH ...
I KNOW! START-ING TODAY...
...YOU CAN BE THE HEALTH COORDI-NATOR!
HUH?

BAM
CLINIC
HUH?
CLINIC
BAM
AIIE-EEE!
BAM
HUH?
FLU SHOTS AVAILABLE TODAY
I'll dieeeee!
Nooooo! I'm going home!
Murder-rrrr!!
HUH?!
HOWL HOWL

WELL, WELL, YUIGA!
THEY'VE ROPED YOU INTO BEING THE HEALTH COORDINATOR NOW, HUH?
GRIN
WELL, ASUMI, LOOKS LIKE YOU'LL BE SEEING MORE OF YUIGA, ON AND OFF THE CLOCK! ♡
HOWL HOWL
...
!
NOOOOOO!! NO SHOT!! NOOOO!
HEY NOW ...
KOSUKE...
TENSE TENSE
BE A GOOD BOY AND SETTLE DOWN NOW...
OKAY?
THIS WON'T HURT...
OH!
SMAK
SHOOP
YOU'RE LYING!
HEY!
KOSUKE...
WAIT ...
WAIT

IT'LL HURT FOR SURE WITH SUCH A NERVOUS DOCTOR!
YOU'RE NO GOOD, ASUMI!
WHAT ?!
Bwa ha ha
SHOOOSH
HEY, HOLD IT RIGHT THERE, YOU KIDS!
What do you think you're doing?!
TMTMP TMP TMP
RUN! RUN!
IF THEY CATCH US, WE'LL GET SHOTS!
...
Sheesh...
S-SENPAI... ARE YOU OKAY?
!
TUG
IT'S ALL RIGHT, YUIGA...

PSST...

IT'S A GOOD LEARNING EXPERI-ENCE.

THIS IS DIFFERENT FROM WHAT SHE LEARNED IN MED SCHOOL.

NOW SHE HAS REAL HUMAN PATIENTS.

DEALING WITH REAL PEOPLE...

...IS DR. ASUMI'S FIRST STEP.

DEALING WITH...

...REAL PEOPLE...

BZZZ

BZZZ

BZZZ

BZZZ

BZZZ

BZZZ

Ike
TOIKEYA
SNACKS • TOYS TEL(00)0000
FUKASHIGI STORE
ミルクキャラメル
アイスクリーム

YIKES! IT'S SENSEI! RUN!
FWSH
HOLD UP, GUYS!

SENSEI! YOU'RE COOL!
HOW'D YOU DO THAT?!
IT'S ALL ABOUT COLLECTING THE AIR AT THE BOTTOM OF THE WRAPPER.
I CAN DO THAT!
Hmph!
SPLAT
?!
GROWING UP, MY FAMILY WAS POOR...
...SO WHEN WE GOT TREATS LIKE THIS, IT WAS SUPER SPECIAL!

YOU WERE A KID ONCE, SENSEI?
OF COURSE.
AND I HATED SHOTS TOO.
HONESTLY, I'M STILL NOT WILD ABOUT THEM ...

WIMP... AND YOU'RE A GROWN-UP.
Huh...
Ouch!
GROWN-UPS ARE PEOPLE TOO, YOU KNOW!

AND AS A PERSON...
...I WANT YOU KIDS TO KNOW ME BETTER.
AND I WANT...
...TO KNOW YOU BETTER TOO.

I'M HOME ...
SHOOSH

WELCOME HOME, DARLING! ♡
YOUR DINNER AND BATH ARE READY...
...AND THE HOUSE IS SPARKLING CLEANY-POO! ♡
SPARKLE ♡
WHAA-AAT?! S-S-SEN-PAI?!
YOUR MAID OUT-FIT?!
This is my apartment, isn't it?!
DA DA DADADUM
LIKE I SAID, IT'S EMBAR-RASSING, BUT I PROMISED!
ANYWAY, I THINK I'VE STILL GOT IT GOING ON, RIGHT?
Tee hee!♡
THAT'S WHAT YOU MEANT BY SHOW-ING YOUR APPRE-CIATION?!

SHE'S MORE GROWN-UP NOW THAN BEFORE...

...AND SOMEHOW EVEN SEXIER.

BADMP BADMP BADMP

BLUSH

HM? WHAT'S UP, KO-HAI?

YOU DON'T SEEM DISPLEASED!

Heh!

WHAT?!

I-I DON'T KNOW WHAT YOU'RE TALKING ABOUT!

WELL, I WAS REALLY HOPING YOU'D LIKE IT...

SHOOSH

KO-HAI...

BADMP

HUH?

YOU SAW WHAT HAPPENED THIS AFTERNOON!

I'VE GOT TO PROVE MYSELF AS A DOCTOR AS SOON AS POSSIBLE!

AAAAH

EEEK! BUT NOT LIKE THIS!

DA DA DA DUM
DON'T WORRY. I WON'T HURT YOU. ♡
SENPAI, YOU FEEL SO SOFT...
AAGH! NO! I MEAN, YOUR EYES ARE SCARY!
TREMBL
!
TENSE
TENSE

ARE YOU AFRAID...
...OF REAL HUMAN PATIENTS ...
...SEN-PAI?

THE NEXT DAY...
YOU KIDS...
CLINIC
...ARE NOT GETTING AWAY TODAY.
BAM
YIKES!
YIKES!
WAH!
No way! Rats!
Noooo!
WAA-AAAH!
I HATE SHOTS!!
FWOO FWOO
FWOO FWOO
KOSUKE...
!

I HEARD ...
...THAT YOU KNOW OF A GREAT FISHING SPOT.
WOULD YOU MIND SHOWING ME SOMETIME?
DO YOU LIKE FISHING TOO, ASUMI SENSEI?
DO YOU LIKE BOAT FISHING OR SHORE FISHING?
PRICK
THERE. ALL DONE.
OH!
?!
WHAT ?!
TEE HEE HEE!
THAT DIDN'T HURT AT ALL!
RE-MEMBER, WE'RE GOING FISHING TOGETH-ER, FOR REAL! ♪
DADADADA
I THOUGHT KOSUKE HATED SHOTS!
DUM
WELL, MAYBE IT DOESN'T HURT SO MUCH AFTER ALL.
MASAO, I HEAR YOU'RE BIG ON BARBE-CUING.
YEAH! I GOTS THIS LEG-ENDARY SAUCE, SEE...
PRICK
WHAT KIND OF MAGIC DID YOU USE?

JUST A LITTLE ...
...INNO-CENT CHIT-CHAT!
SENPAI...

KOSUKE LOVES FISHING.
YOU CAN REALLY GET HIM GOING ON AND ON ABOUT BAIT OR HIS SECRET SPOT.
MASAO LOVES TO BARBECUE AND HAS HIS OWN LEGENDARY HOMEMADE SAUCE.
SA-YAKA'S A FULL PURE FAN...

THANK YOU FOR TELLING ME, KOHA
BUT I DON'T KNOW IF THAT MAKES IT LESS SCARY.
WELL, I'M NOT A DOCTOR ...
...SO I DON'T REALLY KNOW HOW SCARY IT IS...
...TO FACE REAL HUMAN PATIENTS.
BUT I DO KNOW ONE THING.

I KNOW HOW CAPABLE YOU ARE...
...AT SINCERELY CONNECTING WITH PEOPLE...
JOLT
JO
...AND GENUINELY MAKING THEM SMILE.
SO I THINK IT'S FINE IF YOU'RE SCARED.
YOUR FEAR...
...JUST PROVES HOW MUCH YOU CARE ABOUT YOUR PATIENTS.
THAT'S MUCH BETTER THAN A DOCTOR WHO KNOWS NO FEAR FROM THE START.
AND BECAUSE THAT'S HOW YOU ARE...
...WHEN YOU GENUINELY MAKE A CONNECTION WTIH SOMEONE...
...I KNOW YOU CAN FIND A WAY TO EASILY HANDLE THAT FEAR AND THAT PRESSURE!

SHEESH...
THAT KOHAI...
...IS TOO BIG FOR HIS BRITCHES SOMETIMES.
RUMMAGE
BUT...
WELL...
I GUESS...
...IT'S TRUE THAT...
...I FEEL KINDA SAFE...
...AROUND HIM.
...MAYBE TONIGHT...
...I'LL WEAR MY NURSE OUTFIT.

TAICHI
NAO
KOSUKE
MASAO
SAYAKA

Question 171: [X] =Tomorrow Night's Pixie, Part 3

HEY, KIDS

DON'T GO OUT TOO FAR!

YES, ASUMI SENSEI!
THANK YOU, KOMINAMI SENPAI.
I APPRECIATE YOU HELPING OUT TODAY, EVEN THOUGH YOU'RE BUSY...
IT'S FINE.
SUPERVISING KIDS IS GOOD EXPERIENCE!
IGHT ...
GLEAM
GLEAM
SHINE
SHINE

WHSH
BADMP
BADMP
Hey, there
That's
too fa
YOU WERE CHECKING ME OUT JUST NOW, WEREN'T YOU...
MUTTR
JOLT
...PERVY SENSEI? ♡

I WAS NOT!
AND WHO ARE YOU CALLING PERVY SENSEI?!
OH! IS YUIGA SENSEI PERVY?!
WHAT'S "PERVY," SENSEI?!
NO!
IT'S NOT A WORD YOU NEED TO KNOW!

Let's go swimming, Pervy Sensei!
I can't swim...and don't say "pervy"!
Tee hee hee!
...
GEE...

THIS STINKS.

I USED TO BE THE LEADER!

BUT NOW EVERYONE'S INTO YUIGA SENSEI, HUH?

ARE YA KINDA LONELY, TAICHI?

SHUT UP, NAO!

ALSO, HE'S WEIRDLY CHUMMY WITH ASUMI!

I DON'T LIKE THAT YUIGA CREEP!

STUPID MAIN-LANDER...

Gah!

WELL, ASUMI SENSEI'S A MAIN-LANDER TOO.

YOU'RE JUST JEAL-OUS.

HEY, I JUST HAD AN IDEA!

YOU CAN HELP ME, NAO!

DA DA DA DA DUM

YOU DIDN'T HEAR A WORD I SAID...

SEN-SEI!

!

WHAT IS IT, NAO?!

Huff! Huff!

COME QUICK, SENSEI!

IT'S TAICHI!

HE GOT HURT IN THE CAVE BY THE INLET!
?!
WHA ... WHAT ?!

I DIDN'T KNOW THERE WAS A CAVE HERE...
THANK YOU FOR SHOWING US.
THE VICE-PRINCIPAL IS WITH THE REST OF THE KIDS.
PLEASE GO BACK AND JOIN THEM, NAO.
...

HEH HEH HEH!
IT'S WORKING, NAO!
SHOOP
...

TAICHI, I DON'T THINK THIS IS A GOOD IDEA...
DON'T BE A SCAREDY-CAT, NAO!
YOU'RE THE ONE WHO SAID YUIGA WAS DERPY!
WATCH THIS...
Heh heh heh!
WE'LL SCARE HIM GOOD AND ASUMI WILL SEE WHAT A WIMP HE REALLY IS!
...
I KNEW IT. YOU'RE JUST JEAL-OUS.

TAI-CHI!
WHERE ARE YOU?!
AN-SWER ME!
TAI-CHI!
HOW FAR IN DID HE GO?
DO YOU THINK HE COULD BE UNCON-SCIOUS?
IF SO, WE CAN'T WASTE ANY TIME...
SNEAK
SHOOF
TAKE THAT!

SPLAT

HRK ?!

YEAH! GOT HIM WITH SOME YAM JELLY RIGHT IN THE NECK!

THAT'LL MAKE HIM TOTALLY FREAK OUT, THAT WUSS...

OH!

LURCH

HUH?

BOOOSH♥

?!

...
PLIP
...
HEY, KOHAI...
SO...TAKING ADVANTAGE OF THE DARKNESS...
WELL, WELL!
YIKES!

NO! I'M SORRY, SENPAI!
I FELT SOME-THING SOFT...
DA DA DA DUM
SOFT?!
OH, NOW YOU'RE JUST GOING FOR IT, FULL-ON PERV-DOG STYLE, HUH?
AUGH!
NO! I DIDN'T MEAN...

TH-THAT CREEP! THIS WASN'T SUP-POSED TO HAP-PEN...

FINE! NEW PLAN!

There's more?

Taichi!

Taichi!

MY TRIP WIRE TRAP.

NOW SHE'LL REALLY SEE WHAT A LOSER HE IS!

HE'LL OTALLY LOSE FACE.

Eek!

o disap-pointing How ncool!

VRRK

BOING
WHOA!
WHA—?!
?!
SQUISH
OOG!
SQUISH
CUDDLE
CUDDLE
YEAH, BUT...
DON'T WIGGLE SO MUCH, SENPAI...
RATS! I GOT ASUMI TOO!
BAD EXECUTION...
GRR
GRR
GRR
YOU SEEM TO BE SCORING A LOT OF BENEFITS HERE, KOHAI!
WHAT?!

QUIT BEING SO COZY TOGETH-ER!
BAM
TAI-CHI?!
AA-AAUGH! WHOOPS!
I DIDN'T MEAN TO!
Taichi, you dope!
TAICHI? I THOUGHT YOU WERE INJURED...
NAO, YOU TOO?
?!
WHAT'S GOING ON? IS THIS SOME KIND OF JOKE?!
RIP RIP
SH ...
SHUT ...
SHUT UP!
WHSH
I HATE MAIN-LANDERS, YOU JERK!
OH!
!
TAI-CHI!
WATCH OUT! WE SHOULDN'T GO TOO FAR...
KRAKK

AH...

KLUNKA KLUNKA

SHAAAA

AAAAAAAAH!

TAI-CHI!

NGH!

HEY! LET GO OF ME, NAO! YOU...

TAI-CHI!

SHOOSH

TAI-CHI!

SHUP

NAO!

GRAB

?!

GRAB

S...

ROLL ROLL ROLL

SENSEI?!

RRUMBLE RRUMBLE

CRASH

SLIP
WAH!
WAH!
WAH!
SOB!
OH NO!
IT'S ALL RIGHT.
THEY FAINTED, THAT'S ALL.
ARE YOU ALL RIGHT, TAICHI?
Phew...
OH NO! IT'S ALL MY FAULT!
WAAAH!
OH NO!
ASUMI AND NAO!
YES... W-WHEN...
WHEN I FELL...
YOU AND ASUMI PROTECTED ME...
BUT...

OH, GOOD.
THAT'S A RELIEF.
WHAT ABOUT SENSEI?
IS HE OKAY?
WELL THEN, LET'S GET GOING.
HUP
CAN YOU GET NAO, TAICHI?
HUH? GO WHERE?
WELL, WE'VE GOT TO GET BACK OUT.
SEE HOW THE ROCK IS A DIFFERENT COLOR DOWN HERE?
WHEN THE TIDE COMES IN, WE'LL BE UNDER-WATER.
I CAN'T SWIM, SO THAT'S GAME OVER FOR ME!
DOESN'T LOOK LIKE WE CAN CLIMB OUT THE WAY WE FELL IN.
HOPE-FULLY THERE'S ANOTHER WAY...
S...
SEN-SEI...
AREN'T YOU MAD AT ME?

WELL, YOU'RE ALREADY SORRY, RIGHT?

NOD NOD
NOD
YES.
YES!
THEN WE'RE GOOD.

WHEN A STUDENT MAKES A MISTAKE...
...HELPING THEM UNDER-STAND HOW TO NOT MAKE THE SAME MISTAKE AGAIN...
...IS THE TEACHER'S JOB.

SO, TAICHI...
IF YOU'RE A LEADER...
...THEN YOU SHOULDN'T TAKE ADVANTAGE OF THE KIDS WHO FOLLOW YOUR LEAD.
YOU SHOULD BE A GUY WHO CAN TAKE CARE OF PEOPLE, RIGHT?
YES, SENSEI!
...
UM, SEN-SEI?
DO YOU WANT TO BE A GUY...
...WHO CAN TAKE GOOD CARE OF ASUMI?!

YES.
I'D LIKE THAT.
SHE'S ALWAYS BEEN...
...SOME-ONE I REALLY CARE ABOUT.

YOU'RE COOL, SENSEI!
IF I'M NOT THE ONE, I THINK I CAN TRUST YOU TO TAKE GOOD CARE OF ASUMI!
IF YOU EVER NEED A GUY TO TALK TO ABOUT ROMANTIC STUFF, I'M HERE FOR YOU!
DA DA DA DUM
WHAT ARE YOU TALKING ABOUT?!

You naughty thing!

Nao, we were so worried!

Oh, Nao, I'm so glad you're okay!

SEN- ... SEI...

!

NAO?

I'M SORRY...

...FOR CAUSING TROUBLE...

...AND...

...FOR CALLING YOU DERPY.

AND...

ALSO...

THANK YOU...

GLANCE

I'm sorry! I'm sorry!

...FOR SAVING TAICHI.

WHOA!
BE CAREFUL! DON'T FALL NOW, SENPAI!
SPLASH
SPLASH
OH, IT'S FINE! WE BARELY SWAM ALL DAY!
IT'LL STING YOUR CUTS!

TEE HEE! ♪
I DON'T CARE!
?
SENPAI'S REALLY IN A GOOD MOOD.
SHE MUST REALLY LOVE THE OCEAN, HUH?
Good thing it's so close.
BY THE WAY...
...WHAT DID YOU MEAN BY WHAT YOU SAID?
WHAT I SAID?
WHAT ARE YOU TALKING ABOUT, SENPAI?
OH, NOTHING!

After I went to all the trouble of wearing a swimsuit...
...I get no love!
BOING
YUKARI SHIMA
Whoa...
Are you really in junior high?
AI HIMURO

Question 172: [X] = Tomorrow Night's Pixie, Part

Question 172: [X] = Tomorrow Night's Pixie, Part 4

MM...

zzZ

zzZ

HUH?! KOMINAMI SENPAI?!

WHY ARE YOU SLEEPING AT MY PLACE?!

DADADADUM

Huh?!

WHA-?!

OH, SHOOT! I MEANT TO WAKE YOU UP, BUT I FELL ASLEEP TOO!

WHAT WERE YOU THINKING?
TEE HEE!
DID THAT MAKE YOUR HEART RACE?
!
WELL, ANYWAY! TODAY'S THE...

BADMP

YIKES! WHERE'S MY HEAD AT?!

BLUSH

IT'S TOTALLY THAT DREAM'S FAULT...

ARE YOU LISTENING, KOHAI?

BA DMP BA DMP

Y-YES! SORRY!

?

HEY, YOU'VE GOTTA PULL IT TOGETHER TODAY!

AFTER ALL, TONIGHT'S ...

BAM
やきとり
ベビーカステラ
...THE ISLAND'S BIG...
...ANNUAL FESTIVAL!
KAREI ISLAND SCHOOL BOOTH
MAID-CHAYA
MAID TEA HOUSE
IT'S A MAID TEA HOUSE!
ガリオレ
300円
ビール
えだまめ
サイダー
メロンソーダ
コーラ
オレンジ
かき氷
氷
オムライス 500
KAREI ISLAND SCHOOL BOOTH
MAID-CHAYA
MAID TEA HOUSE

A MAID CAFE...?
ISN'T THAT KIND OF RISQUÉ FOR A SCHOOL-SPONSORED BOOTH?
It's "Maid Tea House"!
HA HA!
THE STUDENTS CHOSE IT. I DON'T MIND.
ANYWAY, YUIGA SENSEI, I'M VERY IM-PRESSED ...
...AT YOUR ABILITY TO WHIP UP THESE COS-TUMES!
How do I look?
SEN-SEI!
OH...
SHIM
...AND HIMURO!
HUH? SHIMA, YOU LOOK DIFFERENT SOMEHOW...
OH, WELL...
HA! YOU NOTICED, SENSEI? ISN'T YUKARI SUPER CUTE?!
SHE'S EVEN CUTER WITH HER BANGS PINNED BACK, RIGHT?!
YES, VERY CUTE.
JOLT
SHOOP
Heyyy!
WELL, WELL ...

MAID-CHAYA
MAID TEA HOUSE
WHAT A SMOOTH TALKER YOU ARE, KOHAI!
SENPAI AND MS. KASUMI!
YOU'RE HERE!
WE WERE HAVING A LOOK AROUND...AND THOUGHT YOU'D NEED SOME HELP.
SINCE IT WAS MY IDEA AND ALL.
The Maid Tea House!
I ALWAYS WANTED TO EXPERIENCE A MAID CAFE! ♡
Whoaaa!
Well, when it comes to maids, I'm a pro...

WHSH
OH!
THANK YOU!
WHY DOES MY MIND KEEP GOING THERE?!
?
SURE, BUT WHAT'S UP?
Why are you all flustered?

GOSH, WE'RE NOT GETTING ANY CUSTOMERS.
Despite the foot traffic...
MAID TEA HOUSE
IT'S TRUE...
COULD BE PEOPLE AREN'T INTO THE MAID TEA HOUSE THING...

MAYBE THEY'RE STILL BEING WARY OF OUTSIDERS!

HUH?

YEAH.

YUIGA SENSEI AND ASUMI SENSEI, YOU'RE BOTH NEW TO THE ISLAND...

Sheesh!

BUT WHO CARES IF YOU'RE MAINLANDERS!

WHAT MATTERS IS WHAT'S ON THE INSIDE!

LOOK WHO'S TALKING, TAICHI...

...

OOOKAY!

I HAVE AN IDEA!

MAID TEA HOUSE!

HERE! ♡

WHY DON'T YOU TWO GO TAKE A LAP AROUND THE FESTIVAL AND ADVERTISE THE BOOTH?
IT'LL BE A GOOD CHANCE FOR THE ISLANDERS TO GET FAMILIAR WITH YOUR FACES!
HEH!
TRUE... WELL...
Glance
Glance
I DO FEEL SOME DISTANCE FROM THE IS-LANDERS ...

OKAY! WE AREN'T HERE TO HAVE FUN!

WE'VE GOTTA GET THE WORD OUT...

Maid Tea House!

Please stop by!

HEY, KOHAI!

WANT SOME?
THE CHOCO-LATE BANA-NA'S MINE!

YOU'RE TOTALLY ENJOYING THE FESTIVAL
BAM
What about our job?
WHAT?
OH, COME ON. CAN'T WE HAVE A LITTLE FUN?
We passed out all the flyers!
TODAY'S SPECIAL ...
...SO LET'S HAVE A DATE!
D-DA–
SPEAK-ING OF WHICH ...
SHOOOF
MFF ?!
HOW COME YOU CAN SAY THAT TO YOUR STU-DENTS...
...BUT YOU NEVER...
...SAY THOSE THINGS TO ME?

HUH?
SAY WHAT TO MY STUDENTS?!
JUST KIDDING!
TMP
ONCE AGAIN, I'M JOKING!
JOKING! ♪

MORE IMPORTANTLY, DID YOU NOTICE...
...THE INDIRECT KISS?
MWA ♡

WHAT?!
TEE HEE HEE!
ENJOY! ♡
SHEESH!
I'M A GROWN-UP—AN INDIRECT KISS IS NO BIG DEAL!
GOLDFISH GAME
BADMP BADMP
I MEAN, WE'VE ALREADY...
...KISSED PLENTY OF TIMES!
GASP

...
I...

KOMINAMI CLINI
WHAT IF...
...WE REALLY DO END UP TOGETH-ER?

I THINK IT ALL START-ED...
...WITH THAT KISS.
AND BE-FORE I KNEW IT, LIT-TLE BY LITTLE...

UM, SENPAI?

DOHA-CHAN LAND INVITATION

I WAS WONDERING...

...IF YOU'D LIKE...

...TO GO HERE TOGETHER.

AROUND THAT TIME...
I...
...STARTED TO FALL...
...FOR ASUMI KOMINAMI SENPAI...
SHOOSH
HM?
WHAT'S UP, KOHAI?
YOU PERVING OUT AGAIN?
N-NO WAY!
KRASH
!
OW ...
NNGH ...
OH!
HUH?

THE OLD ICE SELLER THREW OUT HIS BACK!
NGH...
SOME-ONE, CALL A DOCTOR!
!
RATS...
I NEED TO GET THIS TO THE SHAVED-ICE STAND RIGHT AWAY...
QUIVER QUIVER
ARE YOU OKAY?!
!
MAY I TAKE A LOOK, GRAND-PA?
NO!
BACK OFF, MAIN-LANDERS!
SCOWL
NO ISLANDER WOULD ACCEPT HELP FROM A MAIN-LANDER!
NOOOOOO!!
KRAK KRAK KRAK KRAK
KRUNCH
GRANDPA!!
WHAT DO YOU THINK YOU'RE DOING, MAIN-LANDER?!
JUST BECAUSE HE'S THE ISLAND'S WORST OLD GROUCH...
DA DA DA DA DUM

I'M ALL BET-TER!
WHAAT?!!
NOW, GRAND-PA...
NO CARRYING HEAVY LOADS FOR A WHILE.
That was just first aid.
YEE-EOW-CH!
DID YOU HEAR ME?
QUIVER
QUIVER
HOIST
MMPH...
?!

WHO
!
NGH
THIS IS SUPER HEAVY...!
G-GIVE THAT BACK, PUNK!
I DON'T NEED A MAIN-LANDER'S HELP...

I'VE ONLY BEEN ON THE ISLAND A FEW MONTHS, BUT...
...IT'S A GREAT PLACE!

SO...
IF YOU JUST ALLOW ME TO REPAY A BIT OF MY DEBT OF GRATITUDE TO THE ISLAND...
...IT WOULDN'T COMPROMISE ISLANDER PRIDE...
... WOULD IT?
...
...
YOU'VE GOT MORE THAN TEN DELIVERIES LEFT!
BETTER RUN, PUNK!
WHAAAAT?!
Lugging this?
PHEW ...
I DIDN'T EXPECT TO HAVE TO RUN ALL OVER THE FESTIVAL...
WOBBLE
WOBBLE
SO MUCH FOR ADVERTISING. YOU SPENT THE WHOLE NIGHT WORKING FOR FREE...
You worked hard...
AS USUAL, YOU'RE TOO NICE FOR YOUR OWN GOOD—
OH!

SENSEI! ASUMI! WHERE'VE YOU BEEN?!
WE NEED YOU!
KAREI ISLAND SCHOOL BOOTH
MAID-CHAYA
MAID TEA HOUSE
Hurry! Hurry!
?
BAM
KAREI ISLAND SCHOOL BOOTH
MAID-CHAYA
MAID TEA HOUSE
DA DA DA DUM
BUSINESS IS BOOMING?!
WHAT HAPPENED?!
OH!
IT'S OUR HEROES!
TMP TMP
TMP TMP

DA DA DA
DUM
WOW, THAT WAS QUITE A DISASTER, SONNY!
HUH?!
THANK YOU, SENSEI!
I HEAR YOU RESCUED OUR NOTORIOUS OLD GRUMP!
BWA HA HA!
WORD SPREADS FAST ON AN ISLAND, DOESN'T IT?
!
HMPH!
SLRP
SLRRP
WHO'S AN OLD GRUMP?
ME?

HEY, I WANNA BUY A DRINK FOR THE ISLAND'S NEW FRIENDS!
LET'S TOAST THE YOUNG COUPLE!
BLUSH
ER, WE'RE NOT A COUPLE!
OH, AND WE'RE ACTUALLY STILL WORKING...
OH, GO ON! DRINK UP!
FOR REAL?!
BWA HA HA

OOG...
THROB THROB
MY HEAD HURTS...
Kya ha ha!
YOU ONLY HAD ONE DRINK, YOU LIGHT-WEIGHT!
YOU COULD'VE SAID NO!
Here. Water.
Ha ha...
MUST BE GENETIC...
HM?
GENE-TIC?
MY FATHER WAS A LIGHT-WEIGHT TOO.
BUT HE WOULD TRY TO KEEP UP...
...AND TOTALLY PASS OUT!

OH.
BY THE WAY, SEN-PAI...
YOU LOOK GREAT...
...IN THAT OUTFIT.
WHERE DID THAT COME FROM?
I WAS JUST KIDDING BEFORE, YOU KNOW.
IN THAT CASE, SENPAI...

WANNA FIND OUT?
BADMP

SORRY...

I KNOW... WE REALLY ... SHOULDN'T ... BE...
...DOING THIS.

O-O-OH! YOU'RE RIGHT!
GOSH, I'M SORRY!
N-NO...
I'M SORRY!

...
...

SO ... GUESS I'LL GET GOING.
PEOPLE WILL WORRY.
SURE. I'LL JUST GET A BIT MORE AIR FIRST...

SHP

RUSTLE

DOHA-CHAN LAND INVITATION

DOHA-CHAN LAND INVITATION

ドハッちゃんランドご招待券

SNEAK

GOSH...

...THOSE TWO...

WHAT'S GOING ON...

...BETWEEN THEM?

Gasp! Some-where far away, my big brother's in trouble...
I should have gone with him!
Mizuki Senpai, you're so beautiful when you're wistful!
MIZUKI FAN CLUB
MIZUKI NARIYUKI COLLEGE STUDENT

Question 173:
[X] = Tomorrow Night's Pixie, Part 5

[x] We + Never ÷ × Learn

DOHA-CHAN LAND INVITATION
THANK YOU, KOHAI...
...BUT I CAN'T ACCEPT THIS.
YOU KNOW...
...I'M GOING TO BE BUSY WITH SCHOOL.
I REALLY APPRE-CIATE IT.
...BUT PLEASE ...
...INVITE SOME-ONE ELSE.

OOK!
EEK!

AHH...

WHAT A GREAT SECRET...
So full of animals...
IT'S A NICE SURPRISE THAT THERE'S A HOT SPRING OUT HERE IN THE HILLS.
Ahh...
HEY, KID! YOU LIKE BATHS?
IF YOU DO, CHECK OUT THE NATURAL HOT SPRING IN THE WOODS BEHIND MY PLACE!
Huh?
Huh?
IT'S MY WAY OF THANKING YOU FOR YOUR HELP. GO ON!

THAT OLD ICE SELLER...
EVER SINCE THE FESTIVAL THE OTHER DAY...
...IT SEEMS LIKE HE'S ACCEPTED ME AS PART OF THE ISLAND COMMUNITY.
...
THE FESTIVAL...
SORRY...
I KNOW... WE REALLY SHOULDN'T ...
...BE DOING THIS.
EVER SINCE THEN, EVEN AT HOME...
...IT'S HARD TO LOOK HER IN THE EYES ANYMORE...
BLUG BLUG
AAAAAAAH!!
SPLASH
WHAT'S WRONG WITH ME?!
OOK?!
WHY'D I GO AND DO THAT?!
BLUG BLUG
EEK?!
BUT PLEASE ...
...INVITE SOMEONE ELSE.

COME TO THINK OF IT...
...IT STARTED AROUND THEN.
NOTE
SHE AND I STARTED TO GET...
...MORE AND MORE DISTANT.
I GUESS ...
...I GOT A LITTLE CARRIED AWAY...
... SEEING HER AGAIN AFTER ALL THAT TIME APART.
I'VE GOT TO PULL MYSELF TOGETH-ER!
I SHOULD APOLOGIZE PROPERLY FOR THE OTHER DAY...
SPLISH
!
IS THERE SOME-ONE ELSE HERE?
I can't see much without my glasses...
SQUINT
BUT ...
...THERE SHOULDN'T BE ANYONE ELSE.
ONLY MY FAMILY KNOWS ABOUT IT.
IT'S A SECRET SPOT, SO YOU CAN RELAX.
THAT'S WHAT THE OLD MAN SAID.
MUST BE ANOTHER MONKEY OR SOME-THING...
FWAH

DADA
DA
DA DUM
K-K-KOHAI?!
W-W-WHAT ARE YOU DOING HERE?!
S-S-SENPAI?!
I MIGHT ASK YOU THE SAME!!
SPLOOSH
WELL, IT DOESN'T MATTER!
SPLASH
I'M SORRY! I'LL GO!
HUH?
MY CLOTHES ...
POOF
EEK EEK EEK
!
Give those back!!
OOK!
THE MONKEYS!
EEK!
QUICK, HIDE!
BLOOSH
GLRFF?!

H-HELLO...
DAZE...
HOW'S THE WATER, ASUMI SENSEI?
?!
THOSE VOICES ...
IS IT SHIMA AND HIMURO ?!
BLUG
HUH? I THOUGHT I HEARD VOICES!
OH, WELL...
JUST CHATTING WITH THE MONKEYS, YOU KNOW...
Ook!
GUGUH
WHY ARE THOSE THREE HERE?!
GUH
!!

PSST
PSST
UNLESS YOU WANT TO EX-PERIENCE SOCIAL DEATH, DON'T YOU DARE LOOK, KOHAI!
I WON'T LOOK EVEN IF IT KILLS ME...
GO DEEPER!
AUGH! YOU'RE TOO CLOSE!
GUH
GUH
GLUB
GLUB
YOU'RE TOO CLOSE, SENPAI!
JOLT
HUH ...?
I THOUGHT I HEARD A MAN'S VOICE JUST NOW...
AH HA HA!
THERE'S NO MEN OUT HERE, YUKARI!
Ook!
Eek!
ALMOST NO ONE ON THE ISLAND KNOWS ABOUT THIS PLACE!
IT'S MY GRANDPA'S TOP SECRET SPOT!
Of course, I come whenever I want!
AI HIMURO (14)
HIMURO IS THE OLD MAN'S GRAND-CHILD?!
DOOM
RANDO HIMURO (72)
SO...
You still alive, kōhai?
Gasp
Gasp
Gasp
WHY DID YOU INVITE ME TO YOUR SECRET SPOT?

STARE

OH!

POKE POKE

OH, UM...

I DON'T KNOW IF IT'S OKAY TO ASK THIS, BUT...

MUMBLE

WHAT'S THE STORY WITH...

GLUB

...YOU AND...

...YUIGA SENSEI?

HUH?
I MEAN, THERE'S NOTHING REALLY TO TELL...
OH NO!
I SHOULDN'T BE HEARING THIS!
WHAT I MEAN ...
...IS...

DA DA
IS IT ALL XXX AND OOO, WITH YOU TWO CON-STANTLY XOX-ING AND OXO-ING?
BAAM
AND EVERY NIGHT, DO YOU XOX TILL MORNING AND OXO EACH OTHERS' XXX?
DA DA DA DA
DUM
HUH ?!
BLUSH
I SAID, DO YOU OXO EACH OTHER ON THE XOX?
YUKARI, YOU'RE FREAKING SENSEI OUT!
WELL, AI, YOU TOLD ME TO JUST ASK HER STRAIGHT-OUT...
GLANCE
AAAAAH!
TRY TO KEEP IT IN THE REALM OF AGE-APPROPRIATE CONTENT ...
SHOOSH
I'M AN ADULT, SENSEI!
SO YOU CAN BE HONEST WITH ME!
JOLT
HUH ?!
UH, WE'RE JUST SENPAI AND KOHAI. WE WENT TO THE SAME SCHOOL...

SQUISH♡
SQUISH♡

EEEEK! A RODENT!!
That's cold!
SPLOOSH
BA-BLUG-GA?!

OH! OOPS! KOHAI, I'M SORRY!
You okay?!
NEED... AIR...
AND YOUR CHEST IS TOUCHING MY HEAD...
BLUG BLUG
UM...
ARE YOU OKAY ...?

YOU ...
PSST
... STOPPED THE KISS, RIGHT?
AT THE FESTIVAL...

ASUMI SEN-SEI...
IF YOU DON'T REALLY LOVE HIM...
HEH
...THEN I...
I...
I...I CAN'T HOLD OUT ANY-MORE!!
GLRGG
EVEN IF IT MEANS SOCIAL DEATH...
...I NEED TO BREATHE!!
GRAB
FWAA
?!
Ngh!

W-WHY'D YOU GO UNDER-WATER ALL OF A SUDDEN, SENSEI?!
?!
N-NO REASON ...
SPLOOSH
MORE IMPOR-TANTLY, SHIMA...
...
HM?
TO ANSWER YOUR QUESTION ...

PSST

PSHOO
HUH?!
I... I...
I'M NOT THAT MATURE AFTER ALL!
TMP TMP TMP
YU-KA-RI?!

W-W-WHAT HAPPENED, YUKARI?!
?!
Are we done talking?
SHOOP
...
YOU SURVIVED, KOHAI.
PHYSICALLY AND SOCIALLY.
I-I THOUGHT I WAS A GONER...
PAT
FSHHH

OH...
WHY DIDN'T YOU TELL ME YOU WERE INVITED TO THE HOT SPRING TOO?
I THOUGHT YOU WERE THERE TO SPY ON WOMEN!
NO WAY!
BUT THANK YOU FOR RESCUING ME!
Your clothes are lookin' wild now!
TATTER TATTER

GOSH! TAKING A HOT SOAK WITH ASHUMI!
WHAT A LUCKY DUDE YOU ARE...
...MR. PERVY-PANTS! ♡
P...
PLEASE STOP CALLING ME THAT ...
But it's hard to argue.
TEE HEE HEE! ♪
...
ER...
BACK IN THE POOL ...
THAT KI–
THAT WAS JUST ...
... ARTIFICIAL RESPIRA-TION.
I'M A DOCTOR AFTER ALL.
RIGHT ...

...
I CAN'T SAY IT.

Teruaki Yuiga

I CAN'T TELL HIM...
...HOW I REALLY FEEL.

VRMMM

WE BARELY MADE IT, MISTER!

VRMMMM

SEE THAT BRIGHT-RED SUNSET?

THAT MEANS THERE'S A STORM A-BREWIN'!

A DAY OR TWO LATER, AND I WOULDN'T BE ABLE TO USE THE BOAT!

YOU HERE ON THE ISLAND FOR SIGHT-SEEIN', MISTER?

VRRRM

NO...

I'M HERE TO SEE...

...MY DAUGHTER AND HER BOY-FRIEND!

I'm here to see my brother...
I mean, my boy-friend! ♥
BLUSH
?!
REJECTED DRAFT

Question 174: [X] = Tomorrow Night's Pixie, Part 6

WELL... SINCE KASUMI WAS CALLED AWAY FOR AN EMERGENCY SURGERY OVERSEAS...

...SHE ASKED ME TO COME AND FILL IN!

YAY!

Thanks, Sojiro!

Was Asumi surprised?

Was she?

WHY DIDN'T SHE TELL US? THAT OLD BAG...

WELL...

IN ANY CASE...

Koff!

SHOULDN'T WE THINK ABOUT A DATE FOR THE CEREMONY SOON?

BLRFF

?!

KASUMI TOLD ME EVERYTHING, NARI-YUKIII! ♡
HOW YOU CHASED AFTER ASUMI TO LIVE ON THIS LITTLE ISLAND OUT IN THE MIDDLE OF NOWHERE!
?!
?!
...
ER, SENPAI ...
WHAT ON EARTH ...
PSST PSST
?!
?!
...
I'M SORRY, KOHAI...

THE THING IS...I NEVER MANAGED TO TELL MY DAD...
...THAT WE LIED ABOUT BEING A COUPLE.
WHAAAAAAAT?!
BUT IT'S BEEN QUITE A WHILE SINCE THEN, HASN'T IT?!
DADADA
KOFF KOFF KOFF
I...I'M SORRY!
MY DAD'S HEALTH HAS BEEN PRETTY POOR SINCE THEN.
I WAS AFRAID THAT IF I TOLD HIM, HE MIGHT COLLAPSE FROM THE SHOCK.
DADADADUM
WELL! ISN'T THIS A HAPPY DAY.
REUNITED WITH MY DAUGHTER AND HER PARTNER...
JOLT
!
HEH HEH... SUCH A SPECIAL DAY...
...MAKES ME WANT TO SEE...
...THE LATEST PHOTOS OF YOU TWO SWEET-HEARTS! ♡
BLUSH
DADADADUM

My Beloved

GRIN
GRIN
HO HO!
WELL, YOU SURE SEEM TO BE DOING WELL! ♪
SWIP
SWIP
Huff! Huff! Huff! Huff!
WHAT A PAIR OF LOVE-BIRDS! ♡

Huff! Huff! Huff!
SOME-HOW WE MANAGED TO TAKE THOSE IN A HURRY!
WAY TO HUSTLE, SENPAI!

BUT... WHERE ARE THE PHOTOS OF YOU TWO SHARING A KISS? DON'T YOU HAVE ONE OF THOSE?
HUH?!
DAD, THAT'S ENOUGH! QUIT BEING A PEST!
Mwa!

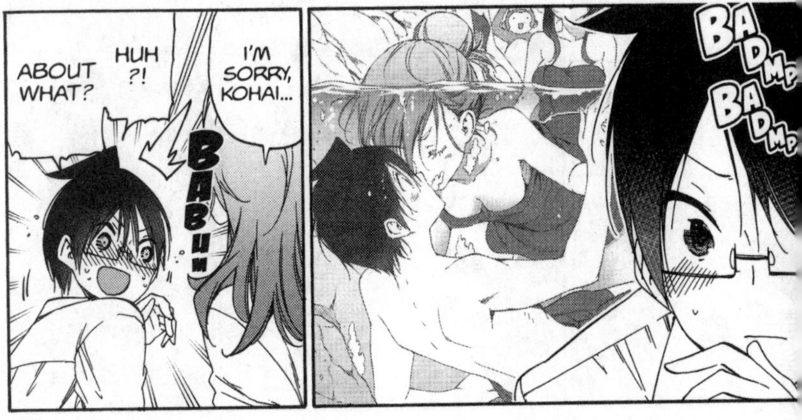

FOR PUTTING YOU THROUGH ...
...YOU KNOW...

WHAT ABOUT YOU, SENPAI?

SHAAA
AT THIS POINT...
...I'VE KNOWN SENPAI FOR YEARS.
BUT I STILL DON'T KNOW HOW SHE REALLY FEELS...
Bye, Sensei!
HOW DOES SHE...
... ACTUALLY FEEL TOWARD ME?
I MEAN ...
SHOOSH
HUH ?!

GOSH, THE RAIN'S REALLY PICKING UP!
ZOOOSH
TAK
TAK
TAK
COME TO THINK OF IT, THE NEWS SAID A TYPHOON WAS COMING...
WAH!

WHAT'LL WE DO, MASAO?
IT'S...
IT'S OKAY, SAYAKA.
WE'LL FIND HIM SOON.

MASAO AND SAYAKA.
YOU TWO SHOULD GO STRAIGHT HOME TODAY.
It's not safe!
OH! SEN-SEI!
YES, WE KNOW!
SPLISH
Bye, Sensei!
OH...

I'M SORRY, NARI-YUKI.

ASUMI CAN BE QUITE A HANDFUL, CAN'T SHE?

HUH?

OH, NOT AT ALL.

SEN...

I MEAN, ASUMI...

...IS REALLY GOOD TO ME...

...AND I...

I'M SORRY.

THE TRUTH IS...

...THERE'S SOME-THING I SHOULD HAVE TOLD YOU A LONG TIME AGO.

OHO.

YOU MEAN...

...ABOUT HOW YOU AND ASUMI...
...AREN'T REALLY A COUPLE?
UH...
BABAM
WHAA-AAT?!
YOU KNEW ?!
WELL ...
THERE'S SOME-THING...
...I SHOULD HAVE TOLD YOU TOO.
NARI-YUKI...

I STILL HAVE REGRETS...
...ABOUT YOUR LATE FATHER.
I ALWAYS WONDER ...
...IF THERE WAS SOME-THING MORE I COULD HAVE DONE.
HUH?
YOUR DAUGHTER'S IN JUNIOR HIGH ALREADY?
KOMINAMI CLINIC
WELL, SHE'S CERTAINLY GROWN!

WHAT DO YOU SAY, YOUNG LADY?
WANT TO MARRY MY SON AND JOIN MY FAMILY ONE DAY?
SHOOP
DON'T BE AN IDIOT, TERUAKI!
I'M NOT GIVING UP MY DAUGHTER TO ANYONE!
OH, COME ON! DON'T BE SO STRICT!
WELL...
SOJIRO...
ABOUT THAT SURGERY...
I'D LIKE YOU TO BE THE ONE TO DO IT.
WE'VE KNOWN EACH OTHER SO MANY YEARS.
I TRUST YOU WITH MY LIFE.
PLEASE.
TERUAKI...

I'M SORRY...
...BUT I CAN'T...
...HELP YOU.
IN THIS LITTLE CLINIC OF MINE...
...I DON'T HAVE THE EQUIPMENT TO TREAT YOU.
I'LL WRITE YOU A REFERRAL TO A UNIVERSITY HOSPITAL WITH STATE-OF-THE-ART FACILITIES.
I UNDERSTAND.
I'M SORRY FOR THE SELFISH REQUEST.
IF THAT'S HOW YOU FEEL...
...I'M SURE I'LL MANAGE SOMEHOW.
BUT...

SHAAAA
IN THE END...
...I...
...WASN'T ABLE TO DO ANY-THING...
...TO HONOR MY FRIEND'S REQUEST.
SOME-TIMES WE DOC-TORS...
...ARE JUST SO POWER-LESS...
WHY ARE YOU...
...TELLING ME ALL THIS...
...NOW?
IF YOU AND ASUMI FOUND EACH OTHER AGAIN ON THIS ISLAND AND EVERYTHING WAS GOING WELL...
...I FIGURED I'D JUST KEEP IT TO MYSELF.
BUT...
I'M SORRY FOR PUTTING YOU THROUGH...
...YOU KNOW...

Teruaki
THAT PATIENT...
...WHO YOU WEREN'T ABLE TO SAVE...
...WAS...
...KOHAI'S FATHER?
Teruaki Yuiga
...HER ACCEPTANCE TO MEDICAL SCHOOL...
ASUMI...
THAT CHART...
WITH HIM...
...I THOUGHT...
...I COULD REALLY...
BUT NOW...
BUT...
I GET IT.
IT'S NOT YOUR FAULT, DAD.
I UNDERSTAND THERE ARE LIMITS...
...TO WHAT YOU CAN DO IN THIS LITTLE CLINIC.

HOW CAN I...
...LOOK HIM...
...IN THE EYE NOW?

EVEN NOW...
...I THINK ASUMI FEELS BAD ABOUT IT.
AND THAT SEEMS TO BE A BARRIER BETWEEN YOU TWO...
I CAN'T ACCEPT THIS...
THAT WAS...
...RIGHT AROUND THAT TIME.

SPLASH
SHP
OH...

SEN-PAI!
OH, ER...
I WAS JUST WONDERING WHAT WAS KEEPING MY DAD SO LONG, SO...
BLUSH
OH!
SHOOOSH
WAIT, SEN-PAI!
SPLASH
PLEASE WAIT, SENPAI!
SHUT UP!
SPLASH
WHY ARE YOU RUNNING AWAY?!
DON'T FOLLOW ME!

YOU'RE ALWAYS ...
...FLIRTING AND TEASING ME...
...BUT THEN...
...YOU ALWAYS END UP RUNNING AWAY FROM ME!

I DON'T ...
...FEEL ANYTHING!
SPLASH
TINK
TINKA
OH ...

TING

SEN-SEI!!
BADMP
!
WHAT'S WRONG ?!
TAI-CHI!
HELP, SEN-SEI!
HUFF!
HUFF!
WE NEED HELP!
IT'S MASAO AND SAYAKA!
BY THE DOCK!
?!
KASPLOOSH
OH, TIGGY!
MEW...
I WAS SO WORRIED ABOUT YOU...
VWOOOO
D-DON'T WORRY. YOU'RE OKAY NOW...
SHIVER
SHIVER
KREAK
SOMEONE WILL COME RESCUE US SOON...
KREAK

BACK IN THE GOOD OL' DAYS...
BZZZ
BZZZ
POP
Hot...
CANDY SHOP
Ice Cream

VWOOOOOO
Question 175:
[X] = Tomorrow Night's
Pixie, Part 7
MA-
SAO
!!
DADADA
DUM
SAYA-
KA!

OH! THOSE DUMMIES ...
WHAT ARE THEY DOING OUT THERE?
STAY BACK, EVERYONE! IT'S DANGEROUS!
WE'LL CALL FIRE RESCUE RIGHT AWAY...
!
I-I'M SORRY, SENSEI !!
I-IT'S ALL MY FAULT!
I-IT WAS MY IDEA TO CHECK OUT THE DOCK...
SAYAKA DIDN'T DO ANYTHING WRONG!
NO! WHAT ARE YOU TALKING ABOUT?!
MASAO WAS JUST TRYING TO HELP ME!
I...
I WAS SO WORRIED...
..BECAUSE TIGGY WAS MISSING.

KREAK
S-SO, IT WAS MY FAULT!
!
KREAK
KREAK
KREAK
!
OH NO!
THAT DOCK'S ABOUT TO GIVE WAY!

TUG
KO...
KO-HAI...
DON'T TELL ME YOU...
DON'T BE STUPID! YOU'LL GET YOUR-SELF KILLED!
YOU CAN'T EVEN SWIM!
IF WE WAIT FOR HELP, IT MAY BE TOO LATE!
I'VE GOT TO...
...RESCUE THEM!
THOSE ARE MY STU-DENTS!

B-B...
BUT YOU...
BESIDES, I TRUST YOU.
IF ANYTHING HAPPENS TO ME...
...I KNOW YOU'LL SAVE ME, SENPAI!
TUG
!
SENPAI?!
YOU CAN'T BRING THEM BOTH BACK ALONE.
BESIDES...

I'M A DOCTOR!

IT'S MY JOB TO PRO-TECT THEM TOO!

THEM AND YOU!

VWOOO

S...

SEN-SEI...

BLRG!

DON'T SLIP, KOHAI!

HOLD TIGHT TO THAT ROPE, NO MATTER WHAT!

SWP
!!
AA-AAH!
SLIP
GRAB

S-SORRY.
AFTER WHAT I JUST SAID...
IT'S OKAY...
LET'S BE CAREFUL, NOW.

WHEN MY DAD DIED...
...HE WAS SMILING.

THAT'S WHY...
...I'M SURE...

...YOUR DAD...
...MADE THE RIGHT CALL.
SO...

IF WE GET BACK SAFE, SENPAI ...

...I HOPE YOU'LL LET ME TELL YOU...

...HOW I FEEL ABOUT YOU.

...
WHERE ARE THOSE FIRE-FIGHTERS?!
WHAT'S KEEPING THEM?!
UM, YUKARI? HELLO?
SOME-THING ON YOUR MIND?
OH... NO. IT'S NOTH-ING!

HERE!
C'MON, KOHAI! YOU TOO! HURRY!
TH...
Huff!
Huff!
BLOOSH
!
OH NO!
KO-HAI!!

SHOOF
HUH?
GASP!
DAD!!
KREAK KREAK KREAK
?!
OH!
HANG IN THERE, NARI-YUKI!
YOU'RE GOING TO BE JUST FINE!
KOFF! KOFF! DR. KOMI-NAMI!

KRASH
DR. KOMI-NAMI!
WATCH OUT!
DAAA-AAD!!
KRASH
KO-HAIIII !!

SHAAA

CLINIC

MURMUR
SOB!
MURMUR
SOB!
SENSEI'S... GONNA BE OKAY... RIGHT, TAICHI?
YEAH!
OF COURSE, NAO!

OUR SENSEI ...
... WOULDN'T DIE THAT EASILY!
THIS ISN'T GOOD ...

SEVERE MUSCULAR GUARDING ...
INTERNAL BLEEDING CAUSED BY A STRONG BLOW TO THE ABDOMEN...
THERE'S PROBABLY SOME INTERNAL DAMAGE.
OH NO ... THEN ...
YES.
HE NEEDS SURGERY RIGHT AWAY TO STOP THE BLEEDING, OR IT COULD BE FATAL.
BADMP
SURGERY!
BADMP
BADMP
BADMP
BADMP

DON'T BE SCARED...

DON'T BE SCARED...

I HAVE TO STAY CALM AND JUST FOCUS ON ASSISTING MY DAD.

IT'S OKAY
SO LONG AS MY DAD'S WIELDING THE SCALPEL, KOHAI'S DEFINITELY IN GOOD HA–
TING

DAD?
Huff!
Huff!

OH!
Y- YOUR ...
... ARM ...

YES...

IT'S BROKEN.

ASUMI...

PLEASE BRING ME A SPLINT.
I CAN STILL MOVE MY FINGERS.
IF I SECURE IT REALLY TIGHT AND STOP THE SHAKING, I CAN DO THIS.
WHA...
WHAT ARE YOU TALKING ABOUT, DAD?
YOU CAN'T DO THAT!
OU MIGHT SUFFER ERMANENT DAMAGE...
MY ARM ISN'T IMPOR-TANT NOW!

IF I DON'T DO THIS SURGERY, WHO WILL?!
KASUMI IS AWAY!
THERE'S NO OTHER DOCTOR ON THE ISLAND!
THERE'S NO WAY TO GET HIM TO THE MAINLAND IN THIS STORM!
WE'RE RUNNING OUT OF TIME!
...
IF I...
IF I DON'T ACT NOW ...
IF I DON'T SAVE HIM...
HOW...
HOW WILL I EVER FACE TERUAKI IN THE AFTER-LIFE?
WHEN MY DAD DIED...
...HE WAS SMILING.
NO.
YOU MADE...
...THE RIGHT CALL.
YOU TOOK CARE...
...OF YOUR PATIENT, DAD.
DAD, YOU'VE...

YOU'VE ALWAYS...
...DONE EVERY-THING YOU COULD FOR YOUR PATIENTS!
YES.
THAT DAY...
...MY DAD DID THE BEST HE COULD FOR HIS PATIENT.
RIGHT NOW...
HOW...
...CAN I DO WHAT'S BEST...
...FOR KOHAI?
BE-SIDES ...
...I TRUST YOU.
DAD...

I'LL PER-FORM...

...THE SURGERY!

SHAAAA
CLINIC
CLINIC
Question 176:
[X] ≡ Tomorrow Night's Pixie, Part 8

SHAAA
SEN-SEI...

YOU'LL PER-FORM...
...THE SURGERY?
ASU-MI...
YOU...

...
BADMP
BEING A DOCTOR...
...IS HARD, RIGHT, DAD?
SOMETIMES WE STRUGGLE TO DO OUR BEST IN A SITUATION FULL OF LIMITATIONS...
...AND WE HAVE TO GRAPPLE WITH OUR OWN POWERLESSNESS.
BADMP
BADMP
BADMP
RIGHT NOW...
THE BEST THING I CAN DO FOR KOHAI...
...IS TO SERVE AS YOUR HANDS, DAD.

SO PLEASE, GUIDE ME...

...AND I'LL PERFORM THE SURGERY.

NO MATTER WHAT...

...OUR PURPOSE AS DOC-TORS IS TO SERVE OUR PATIENTS!

OUR PURPOSE AS DOC-TORS...
...IS TO SERVE OUR PATIENTS...

SHAAA

THAT'S IT.
CARE-FULLY...

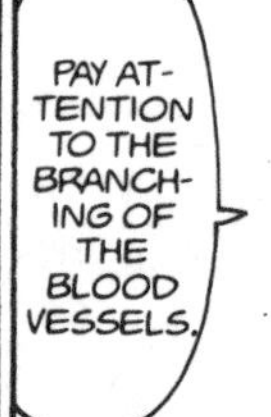
PAY AT-TENTION TO THE BRANCH-ING OF THE BLOOD VESSELS.

R...
RIGHT!
GAH!
BADMP
BADMP

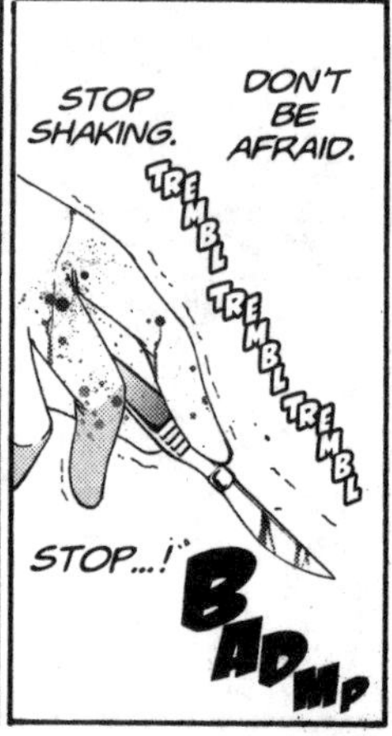
DON'T BE AFRAID.
STOP SHAKING.
TREMBL
TREMBL
TREMBL
STOP...!
BADMP

I THINK IT'S FINE IF YOU'RE SCARED.
JOLT

YOUR FEAR...
...JUST PROVES HOW MUCH YOU CARE ABOUT YOUR PATIENTS.
THAT'S MUCH BETTER THAN A DOCTOR WHO KNOWS NO FEAR FROM THE START.

I KNOW YOU CAN FIND A WAY TO EASILY HANDLE...
...EVEN THAT FEAR AND THAT PRESSURE!

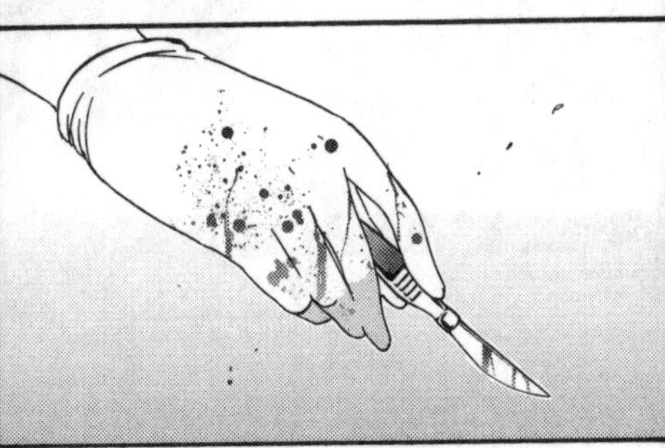

RIGHT...
IT'S NORMAL TO BE SCARED.
ACCEPT IT.

OB-SERVE YOUR OWN FEAR.
AND...
AND THEN...

...FOCUS COM-PLETE-LY...
...ON THE PERSON RIGHT IN FRONT OF YOU.
FOCUS ON KOHAI.
KO-HAI...

MY SEAT'S RIGHT THERE.
CAN I GET BY?
THE FIRST TIME WE MET...
...I THOUGHT KOHAI WAS A DORK.
KOMINAMI CLINIC
UM...
I THINK ASUMI CAN OVERCOME THE CHAL-LENGES!
WON'T YOU GIVE HER A CHANCE? PLEASE?
BUT...
WOW ...
HE CAN BE REALLY SWEET...

WHOA.
HE'S SUR-PRISINGLY MUSCULAR...
ACTU-ALLY...
COME TO THINK OF IT, THIS MIGHT BE THE FIRST TIME...
...I'VE EVER...
BADMP
BADMP
BADMP
BADMP
...BEEN SO CLOSE TO A GUY.
I WON-DER WHEN IT START-ED...
MY DAD WANTS US TO SEND MORE PHOTOS.
I GUESS THERE'S NO WAY AROUND IT...
KOHAI, YOU...
...STARTED TO BE-COME...
...MORE AND MORE IMPOR-TANT TO ME...
SO...
...YOU SEE, KOHAI...

THE TRUTH IS...
...THAT DAY...
DOHA-CHAN LAND INVITATION
...I WAS REALLY HAPPY.
SO HAPPY, I ALMOST WANTED TO CRY.
AND WHEN WE MET AGAIN, ON THIS ISLAND...
...IT SEEMED LIKE FATE.
I WAS SO HAPPY.

WHEN WE SAID GOODBYE, I FELT LIKE I COULDN'T FACE YOU.
BUT EVEN SO...
...I REALLY WANTED TO BE WITH YOU.

IN MY MIND, I KNEW IT WAS WRONG...
I KNEW IT WAS UNFAIR OF ME...
...BUT I REALLY ENJOYED FLIRTING WITH YOU.
I WAS ...
...SO HAPPY TO SEE YOUR REAC-TIONS.
THAT'S WHY...

SORRY ...
...DAD.

I WAS AFRAID THAT IF I TOLD YOU...
...I'D LIED...
...ABOUT US BEING A COUPLE...
...THEN KOHAI AND I WOULD LOSE OUR CONNECTION...
...COM-PLETELY.

I KNEW THAT.
ON SEVERAL OCCA-SIONS...
...YOU CAME CLOSE TO TELLING ME.

HON-ESTLY...

WHEN THE YOUNG MAN YOU PRESENTED TO ME AS YOUR BOY-FRIEND...
...TURNED OUT TO BE TERUAKI'S SON...
...I WAS STUNNED.
IT SEEMED ALMOST...
SHOOP
..LIKE FATE, SOMEHOW.
BUT, YOU KNOW...

I LIKE NARI-YUKI.
NOT AS MY FRIEND'S SON OR AS YOUR BOY-FRIEND...
...BUT SIMPLY...
...AS A HUMAN BEING.

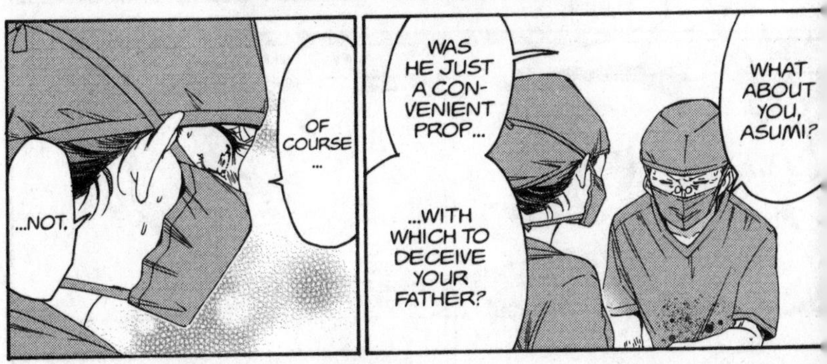
WHAT ABOUT YOU, ASUMI?
WAS HE JUST A CON-VENIENT PROP...
...WITH WHICH TO DECEIVE YOUR FATHER?
OF COURSE ...
...NOT.

THEN, WHO'S TO SAY...
...IF THAT LIE...
...WILL ALWAYS STAY A LIE.

REMEM-BER WHAT I SAID, ASUMI?
I CAME TO THIS ISLAND...

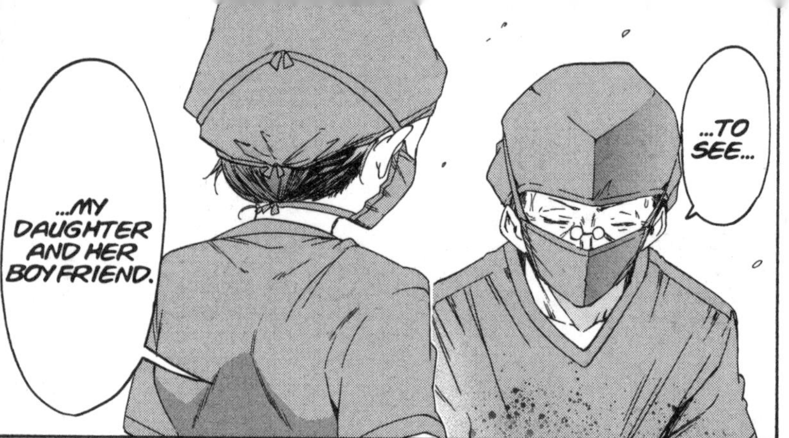
...TO SEE...
...MY DAUGHTER AND HER BOYFRIEND.

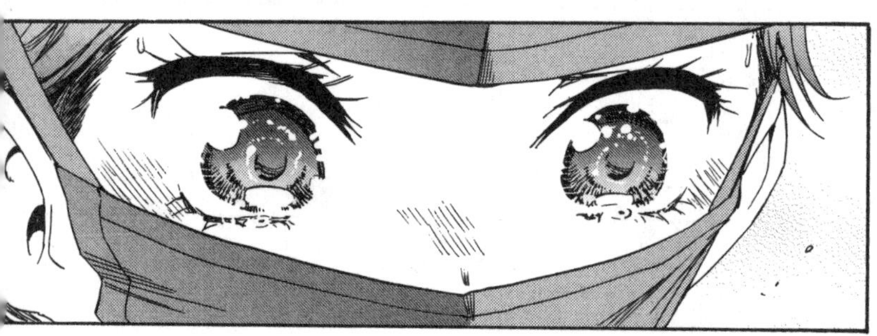

KOHAI...
WHEN YOU WAKE UP...

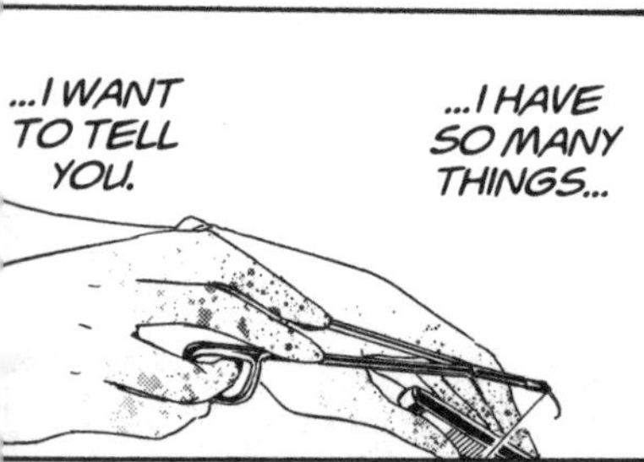
...I HAVE SO MANY THINGS...
...I WANT TO TELL YOU.

I PROMISE NOT TO PLAY GAMES OR RUN AWAY ANYMORE.
SO...
PLEASE, KOHAI...

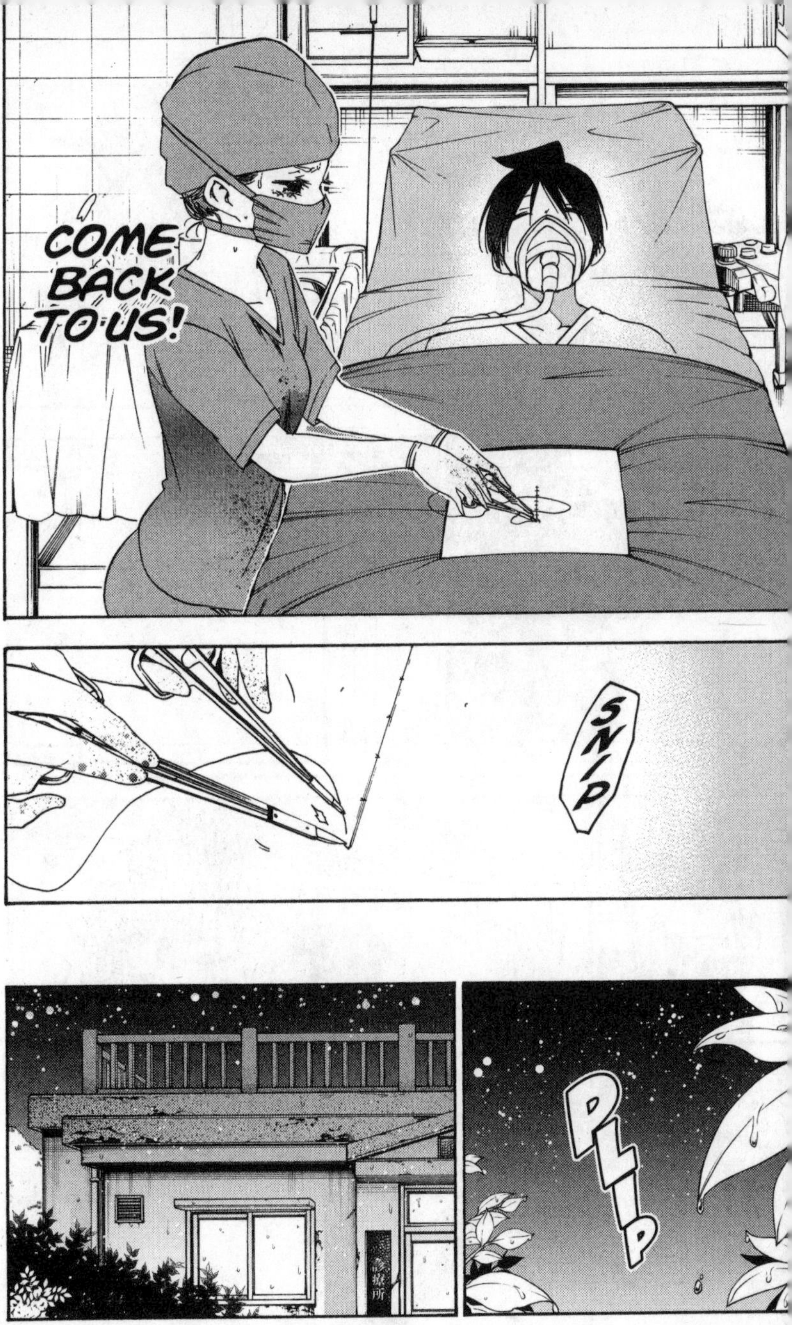

COME BACK TO US!

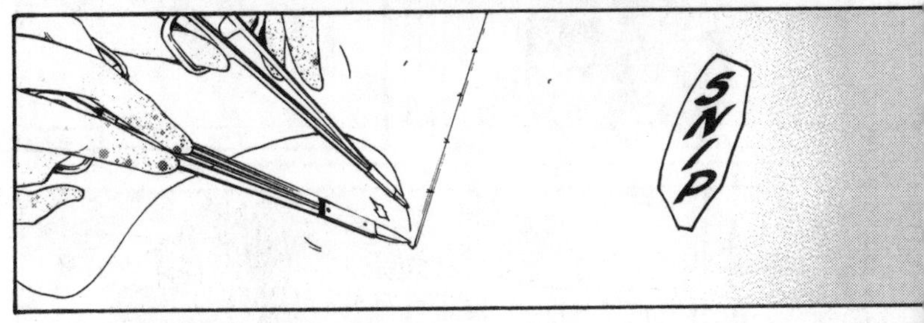

102

RUSTLE

I WAS...
...DREAM-ING JUST NOW...
...ABOUT WHEN WE FIRST MET...
...IN CRAM SCHOOL, SENPAI.

...
ME TOO.
THERE WAS SOME-THING ...
...I FORGOT...
...TO TELL YOU BACK THEN, SENPAI.
HM?
YOU SOUND SO FOR-MAL!
RUSTLE
SEN-PAI...

KCHF
ドハっちゃん
ランド
ご招待券
DOHA-CHAN LAND INVITATION
ASUMI KOMI-NAMI...
...SEN-PAI...

I LOVE YOU.
WILL YOU BE...
...MY REAL GIRLFRIEND?

WHA...
WHAT?
I'M IM-PRESSED, KOHAI...
YOU REALLY...
...TOOK ME BY SUR-PRISE.

SORRY... THAT'S NOT WHAT I MEAN...
HON-ESTLY...
I WAS ABOUT...
...TO TELL YOU...
...
UM...
SO...
WELL...

ALL THIS TIME... I'VE BEEN IN LOVE WITH YOU!

YOU...

STUPID KOHAI!

SO I SHOULD BE THE ONE ASKING...
...IF YOU'RE OKAY WITH IT.
PLEASE... ...LET ME BE YOUR REAL GIRLFRIEND, KOHAI!

Question 177: [X] = Tomorrow Night's Pixie, Part 9

HEY!
WAKE UP, KOHAI!
Bam
OH!
YOU'RE FINALLY AWAKE! ♪
CHIRP
CHIRP
CHIRP
CHIRP
YOUR BREAK-FAST IS READY... ♪
...MASTER! ♡

A-A-ASUMI?!
WHY'RE YOU WEARING A MAID OUT-FIT FIRST THING IN THE MORN-ING?!
WHAT? YOU DON'T LIKE IT?
WOULD YOU PREFER ME IN JUST AN APRON?
Perv!
I-I-I DIDN'T SAY THAT!
DA
DA
DA
DUM

WELL, GOSH... THANK YOU, ASUMI!
IT WAS MY TURN TO MAKE BREAKFAST THIS MORNING...
Yum!
IT'S FINE. I DO IT BECAUSE I ENJOY IT.
BUT HURRY UP AND EAT, OR YOU'LL BE LATE.
OH!
YOU'RE RIGHT! I'VE GOT TO RUN...
THANKS FOR THE FOOD!
KLINK
HEY, NOW. AREN'T YOU FOR-GETTING SOME-THING?
TUG
OH!
MY NECK-TIE...
C'MON, SENSEI. GET IT TOGETH-ER.
NOW, ARE YOU FOR-GETTING ANYTHING ELSE?
N-NO! I'M ALL GOOD!
Thank you...
...very much!
HM?
ARE YOU SURE...
...YOU'RE NOT FOR-GETTING ANY-THING?
FIDGET
...
OH...

SMAK♥
TEE HEE! ♡
COR-RECT! ♡

SEN-
SEI...
CLINIC

SHIMA!
Um...
Um...
GOOD MORNING!
UM... ARE YOUR INJURIES ALL BETTER NOW?
YES.
COMPLETELY!
SEE?
OH...
THAT'S GOOD...
FIDGET
IF ANYTHING HAPPENED TO YOU, SENSEI...
...I DON'T KNOW WHAT I'D DO...
?
Thanks!
HA HA! YOU WORRY TOO MUCH.
Snuggle
IF ANYTHING EVER HAPPENS, BE SURE TO TELL ME...
Hey, missy!
WHAP

?
WAH! W-WHAT ARE YOU DOING?!
DO YOU KNOW HOW LONG I SPENT DOING MY HAIR?!
EEK! EEK!
Muss
Muss
Quit flirt-ing, kid!
YAP
That's my man!
LOOK AT 'EM GO!
PEACE-FUL TIMES...

WE SURE ARE GLAD YER OKAY, YUIGA SENSEI!
Yep, yep!
TRULY!
YES, WHAT A BLES-SING!
RIGHT! LET'S CELE-BRATE YUIGA SENSEI'S RECOV-ERY...
...WITH A PARTY ON THE BEACH TONIGHT!
YEAHHH
HUH?! AGAIN?!
YOU JUST WANT TO DRINK EVERY NIGHT!

BBQ職人
WHEN WAS IT...
...THAT ASUMI...
...TOLD US SHE WAS SERIOUS ABOUT BECOMING A DOCTOR?

I HAD ...
...A HARD TIME ENCOURAG-ING HER.
AFTER TERUAKI'S DEATH...
...SOME-WHERE DEEP INSIDE...
...I ALWAYS HARBORED DOUBTS ABOUT MY-SELF AS A DOCTOR.
DID I REALLY DO THE RIGHT THING?
OUR PATIENTS PUT THEIR LIVES IN OUR HANDS.
I KNEW THAT ONE DAY, MY DAUGHTER MIGHT BE PLAGUED BY SIMILAR QUESTIONS.
SOMETIMES DOCTORS ARE CONFRONTED WITH OUR OWN POWERLESS-NESS.
I DIDN'T WANT MY BELOVED DAUGHTER TO HAVE TO DEAL WITH THOSE DOUBTS...
...
BUT THAT WAS...
...MY OWN SMALL-MINDED EGO.
I NEVER IMAG-INED...
NO MATTER WHAT...
OUR PURPOSE AS DOC-TORS IS TO SERVE OUR PATIENTS!

...MY OWN DAUGHTER...
...WOULD TEACH ME THAT LESSON.
ASUMI IS GOING TO MAKE...
...A FINE DOCTOR.
I...
...SHOULD TRY TO KEEP UP!
HEY, BY THE WAY!
I FORGET... WHAT'RE WE CELEBRATING TONIGHT?
Ga ha ha!
ARE WE CELEBRATING THESE TWO HAVING A BABY?
Heh Heh!
WHAT HAPPENED TO CELEBRATING MY RECOVERY?!
WHAT ARE YOU, CRAZY?!
NO WAY WE'RE HAVING A BABY YET!
Ohhh...
JOLT

"YET" ...?
WOBBLE
!
IN OTHER WORDS ...
YOU PLAN TO IN THE FUTURE?!
DADA DA
THAT'S WHAT IT MEANS, RIGHT?!
WHEN?! A BOY OR A GIRL?!
DADA DA
YOU'LL LET ME NAME IT, RIGHT?!
DUM
WHAT?!
PLEASE CALM DOWN, SIR!
CALL ME DAD!
BAM
UGH! SHUT UP, YOU OLD GOAT!
WE AREN'T EVEN MARRIED YET!
YET?!
BY YET, YOU MEAN YOU...
WHAT'S THIS? YOU'RE GETTING MARRIED, SENSEI?!
AUGH!
THIS IS A GROWN-UP CONVER-SATION! YOU STAY OUT OF THIS!

HON-ESTLY, MY DAD!
HE NEVER CHANGES...
FWA
FWA
HA HA HA!
BUT ...
...IN THE END...
...I KIND OF APPRE-CIATE...
...THAT HE NEVER CHANGES.
KO-HAI ...
HEY...

YOU CALLED ME KOHAI AGAIN...
...ASUMI.

OH ...
OOPS ...
S-SORRY ...
I'M JUST...
...STILL NOT USED TO IT...
NA...
NARI...
...YUKI.

HEH HEH
Heh Heh Heh

AUGH! Y-YOU'RE TEASING ME!
THINK YOU CAN TURN THE TABLES ON ME?!
SHOVE
Y-YIKES!
WHOA!
FWUD

SHAAAA
HEY...
ASUMI...
NARI...

YOU'RE ALIVE.

BADMP

BADMP

I WAS SO SCARED.

THE PRESSURE OF BEING RESPONSIBLE FOR A LIFE IS SO CRUSHING.

LISTEN...

MEDICINE IS NO CAKEWALK!

MY DAD'S WORDS AFFECTED ME SO POWER-FULLY...

...IT WAS PAINFUL.

BUT EVEN SO...

...I'M REALLY GLAD...

...I CHOSE MEDICINE!

THANK YOU.

PLIP

PLIP

FOR LIVING.

THANK YOU!

WILL YOU MARRY ME?

UH...
I WAS THINKING...
...IN THE FUTURE...
...WE COULD RUN THE KOMINAMI CLINIC TOGETHER...
BUT ...
TONK
MOST OF ALL...
...I NEVER WANT...
...TO BE SEPARATED FROM YOU AGAIN, ASUMI!
BACK TO... THAT EARLIER TOPIC...

I...

I'VE FELT...

...THAT I WANT THAT...

... TOO.

YOU MEAN ...
A BAB—

S...
SO...

BUT, YOU KNOW!
ERET
ERET
I'M STILL TRAINING TO BE A PROPER DOCTOR!
THAT'S IN THE FUTURE!
OH, RIGHT! OF COURSE!

Route: 4/5

[*X*] = Tomorrow Night's Pixie

– End –

KOMINAMI CLINIC

HAPPY NEW YEAR, MASHUMI! ♡
IT'S THE YEAR OF THE MOUSE! SQUEAK! ♡
WOW! THERE'S A MOUSE-THEMED EVENT FOR NEW YEARS!
BUT WAIT, SEN-PAI!
I THOUGHT YOU WERE AFRAID OF RODENTS!
SHAKA SHAKA SHAKA
I-I'M FINE. OBVI-OUSLY...
OH! SHE'S HOLD-ING IN HER FEAR!
WHAT A PRO!

RIVER!
SWIM-SUITS!
BARBE-CUE!
WHAT DO YOU THINK OF THIS SWIM-SUIT?
It's... cute.
BOING
Not a swimmer?
AREN'T YOU GOING TO SWIM, SENSEI?
I DE-CLINE.
SUCH DIVER-SIONS ARE FOR CHILDREN.
SZZZ
OH, COME ON. DON'T BE LIKE THAT!
SPLSH

SEE-THROUGH ♥

KIRISU

WHOA! A SCHOOL SWIM-SUIT?!
WOW. HOW DARING, SENSEI...
A-ABSURD!
I BROUGHT THIS BY ACCIDENT!
...
BADMP BADMP

[x] We + Never ÷ × Learn

We Never Learn 20

Taishi Tsutsui

Yu Kato

Sachiko

Yukki

Satoshi Okazaki

Paripoi

Chikomichi

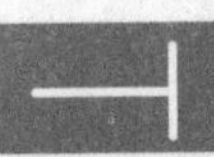

STAFF LIST

[x]
We Never Learn reads from right to left, starting in the upper-right corner. Japanese is read from right to left, meaning that action, word-sound effects and word-balloon order are completely reversed from English order.
1 2 3 4
1 2
5 6 7 8
3 4
9
5
142
Teacher?
現代文B
PLASTIC ERASER
NONO
tempow
100